> I,
> Thank you for what you—
> for children. I hope you get
> some time this Christmas
> for yourself to just "Be."
>
> Grace,
> Al Cad—

GOD'S CALL TO BE:
WHEN BEING PRECEDES DOING

Al Cadenhead Jr.

Smyth & Helwys Publishing, Inc.
6316 Peake Road
Macon, Georgia 31210-3960
1-800-747-3016
©2005 by Smyth & Helwys Publishing
All rights reserved.
Printed in the United States of America.

The paper used in this publication meets the minimum requirements of
American National Standard for Information Sciences—
Permanence of Paper for Printed Library Materials.
ANSI Z39.48–1984. (alk. paper)

Library of Congress Cataloging-in-Publication Data

Cadenhead, Al, 1947-
God's call to be : when being precedes doing
by Al Cadenhead, Jr.
p. cm.
Includes bibliographical references.
ISBN 1-57312-450-8 (pbk. : alk. paper)
1. Christian life—Baptist authors.
I. Title.
BV4501.3.C33 2005
248.4'861—dc22

2005006126

Disclaimer of Liability: With respect to statements of opinion or fact available in this work of nonfiction, Smyth & Helwys Publishing Inc. nor any of its employees, makes any warranty, express or implied, or assumes any legal liability or responsibility for the accuracy or completeness of any information disclosed, or represents that its use would not infringe privately-owned rights.

Contents

Acknowledgments 1
Foreword 3
Introduction: Who in the World Are We, Anyway!? 7

Chapter 1—Being: What Is Underneath? 11
Chapter 2—Being: The Source 21
Chapter 3—Being: A Time of Discovery 27
Chapter 4—Being: Discovering and Sharing Our Best Gift 39
Chapter 5—Being: The Discipline of Waiting 45
Chapter 6—Being: Opening Our Senses 51
Chapter 7—Being: Paying Attention 59
Chapter 8—Being: God Tried to Help Us 71
Chapter 9—Being: Claiming Your Name 81
Chapter 10—Being: Daily Checking the Stock Report 91
Chapter 11—Being: Fatigue, the Silent Opponent 101
Chapter 12—Being: Facing the Giants 107
Chapter 13—Being: The Essence of What It Means to Be 115
Chapter 14—Being: What We Need Most 121

Epilogue 129

*Dedicated to Ashlyn, quite possibly
my best teacher ever on what it means to be.*

Acknowledgments

Special thanks to the gentle and quiet people of Westray, Scotland, who provided the best laboratory possible in the early writing of these pages. Among those special people is my friend Steve Langford, who believed in the possibility of something productive coming from the combination of pen, mind, spirit, and a beautiful island.

My thanks also to Suzanne, who allowed me many evening hours in my study when I could have been tending to other needed tasks.

All Scripture quotes in the following pages are taken from the New International Version.

Foreword
by Chris Cadenhead

"Every time I walk through the doors of this church, I feel torn." The honesty of the woman's words caught me off guard. We were eating at the same table in the fellowship hall on one of our regular Wednesday nights at the church where I serve. Actually, it is better to say we were inhaling our supper at the same table, for the time was fast approaching when everybody would scatter throughout the building for the various activities that happen in the middle of the week.

Planned that night were an adult Bible study, a youth Bible study, choir practice, and at least five different children's ministries I can name. The woman's problem was that she felt a need to be at several of these events all at the same time. Her involvement was requested in numerous places, and she wondered how she could make it happen. And obviously this was not the first time!

I should be quick to point out that she is the kind of church member every pastor dreams of—energetic, creative, deeply committed to the church, passionately in love with God. Yet she is also the kind of church member every pastor can easily abuse—somebody who stands ready to say "yes" every time you ask her to do something.

When you think about it, a situation like this is beyond unfortunate. It is tragic. Church—the place people come to be reminded that they have value because of who they are, to be reminded that they are the recipients of God's unconditional love because He chooses to offer it to them—has become one more place where people are valued because of what they can do. If you can chair a committee, teach a Bible study, organize a mission trip, or lead the music for Vacation Bible School, then the church definitely has a place for you. If you can't, then don't worry. The Nominating Committee will ask you again next year!

The church certainly needs the involvement of people in order to carry out its mission. Ministry cannot happen in a vacuum. But before we throw sign-up sheets and volunteer requests in front of every person who walks through the door, the church is called to meet a deeper need. People need to know God loves and accepts them not because of their abilities or skills, but simply because they are created in God's image. Before God asks any of us to do anything, He asks us to let Him love us. Our deepest need is simply to be in His presence.

In the pages that follow, Al Cadenhead speaks to that deep need. With more than thirty-five years of ministry experience, Al has had the chance to lead and partner with some of the most dedicated workers the church could hope to have. And one would not even want to attempt to tally all the hours he has spent leading and doing. By his own admission, it has all contributed to a career he finds enormously fulfilling. Yet also by his own admission, it has left him wondering: Is there something deeper and more satisfying than accomplishing tasks, even if they are meaningful tasks? And what about those who for whatever reason cannot accomplish great tasks? In a society like ours that measures worth by the standards of productivity and cash value, is there a place to ground the meaning of our lives that is deeper than our fleeting ability to get things done?

As you will see, Al Cadenhead is convinced that the answer is an unqualified "yes." Our lives have meaning and value because of Who created us and what He intends for us. God's great desire is for His creatures to know the joy of being His children, a joy that cannot be earned or achieved or accomplished, only received. Therein lies the thrust of this book: being precedes doing.

This book does not offer an excuse to escape responsibility. Many of the tasks assigned to us in life are important, and we will be held accountable for the commitments we make. What we do matters. But before, behind, and beyond that reality lays the ground of all reality: the God who *is* and who invites us to *be* with Him.

Chris Cadenhead
Senior Pastor
Augusta Road Baptist Church
Greenville, South Carolina

Introduction

Who in the World Are We, Anyway!?

Who are we? More important to me, who am I? This question is far more than philosophical curiosity. There is no sense of triviality when I "square off" with this concern. Instead, the question goes right to the core of a major struggle for me these days. At the time of this writing, I am fifty-seven years old. For most of these years, I have been defined by what I do, especially what I do for a living. Yet the continuous rhythm of the ticking clock is forcing me to face realities that are inevitable for every one of us.

Reality stares back at me every morning when I look in the mirror, and I am reminded that time is doing strange things to me, both internally and externally. Among those realities is knowing that I will not be able to do what I "do for a living" indefinitely. Either due to health, time, or circumstance, there will come a day when how I earn my living will have to change. You may think such an issue is not worth my concern. Yet, my guess is that this issue involves many individuals other than just those who have lived out their lives as ministers.

For thirty-six years of professional life I have focused on some form of ministry, mostly pastoral. Ministry has and continues to be more than a way of providing for my needs and the needs of my family. Ministry is a way of life. The issue becomes more intense when I consider what we refer to as "the call." My response to the call of ministry has been my world. The cap on my head has always proclaimed Pastor, Preacher, Counselor, or Chaplain.

I am a long way from filing for my Social Security, and I cannot even think about annuitizing my retirement fund. If I did that today, I would have to go ahead and file for food stamps. Still, even though I am not walking away from my professional world immediately, I am getting closer, and it seems to be happening much faster than I ever anticipated. The result is that I find myself in the midst of a struggle.

As much as I fear what the final figures of my retirement fund might be, another apprehension looms just as large on the horizon. Stated in one word, the issue has to do with *identity*. When I step out of the pulpit for the last time, give my library away, and turn in my clergy parking pass to the hospital, who will I be at that moment? What will define me when that moment comes?

When you have spent your entire adult life in a particular profession, that profession becomes your primary definition. When I can no longer officially carry the business card of a pastor, what will be printed beside my name? Two issues emerge and etch their way into my mind these days. I confess that, for good or bad, I have willingly allowed my role to define me. Yet, I also want to believe there is more to being me than only that role.

Stated another way, when I peel this familiar, comfortable layer back, will there be anything underneath? In the deep corners of my soul, I believe there is more. But there is mystery to that dimension of my life at this point. Ask me who I am, and I will tell you what I do. I wonder if I am any different from most other people. I can only assume that others must struggle with this same issue.

INTRODUCTION

A Time for Honesty

This issue is so important that I repeat the drill again. If you peel back the professional layer, what is underneath? I feel certain that I will find a layer that points to my role within my family. My family role is certainly not a bad thing, and it adds to my life in huge and dramatic ways. At the same time, I must confess that this role has changed as well. Who I am in regard to my family today is significantly different from what it was fifteen years ago.

More than a decade ago, my family depended on me for the majority of their physical needs. Their housing, food, and transportation were provided by what I, in partnership with my wife, did each day professionally. Through our jobs we made provisions for our needs. Things are different now; while I continue to contribute to my family's physical needs, what I do is not nearly as critical. Our children are married and have lives of their own. They have jobs and provide well for themselves. If needed, my wife is more than capable of providing a means to live. Therefore, even though an important layer of who I am involves my family, I believe there must be more to me than my role as father and husband. I peel back that layer and once again ask, "What is underneath?"

I am sure I would find a layer that shows my tendency to act in slightly obsessive, compulsive ways. I prefer to think of it as being energetic and taking initiative. That sounds nobler than being called hyperactive. Regardless of the label, I have a bit of all these characteristics. To use the language of someone I heard recently, the truth is that I like "doing stuff." I find it challenging. If it is broken, I can fix it. Don't even imply that a service person should be contacted. I find that implication offensive. My wife would accuse me of being too cheap to call for help. I like to think of myself as being resourceful.

Nevertheless, I like *doing*. Giving myself to the activity of doing is one way I express myself. I find great satisfaction in accomplishing a task. However, is my need to fix and repair an indication of my eagerness to correct problems, or is it a sign that I depend on that dimension of my life for affirmation and identification? One of my silent, critical concerns is that I might develop health issues that eventually limit my physical activity. When I can no longer fix and repair, I will face a major identity crisis. It is no laughing matter with me.

The problem, you see, is that when I peel that layer back, like the other layers, I still wonder, "Who is underneath?" Who am I when I am not *doing*? Is there a point in my life when I can find contentment simply in *being*?

If I am honest about this struggle, I believe I will find it is far more than an issue of habits and lifestyle. Somewhere in the mix, I think I must come face to face with who I am in my relationship with God. I have spent most of my life working to please Him. That is a healthy desire, but does my fate with God depend on whether I succeed in pleasing Him? My hunch is that I will discover that He first calls me to be His child before He calls me to do the work of His child.

The following pages are an attempt to share a bit of my own journey. I want to be more than just what I do. If you struggle with that desire in any way, I invite you to join me. We will see where the road leads.

Al Cadenhead

Chapter 1

Being: What Is Underneath?

What is man that you are mindful of him…? —Psalm 8:4a

This book represents a journey that began long before the writing was initiated. I hasten to add that the journey does not end when the final pages are printed. It will continue for the rest of my earthly days. I write because I want a better understanding of some of these issues now, long before the final events occur. The issues to which I refer can best be summarized in a simple question with which I have struggled for a long time. This is the short version: "What is underneath all the usual and routine labels we use as self-identification?" Here's a more detailed version: "Is there more to us than what we do to make provision for ourselves, where we live, what we own, or our family name?" For many of you, this question may seem rhetorical. Let me assure you that it is far more than rhetoric for me. For some time, it has remained in the core of my soul.

A part of my challenge as we begin this journey together is to convey my struggle, including what I think and what I believe, without it sounding like religious rhetoric or overused, "christianized" language. Some of the words may sound routine, but much of the language has taken on new meaning for me. The result is that my struggle and the resulting journey have impacted every dimension of my existence.

I begin by claiming that I am convinced that at the center of my soul is life—not life determined by my heartbeat, but life that comes to me by the Creator God who gives each of us a small but important piece of His divine image. We may be created out of clay, but through that clay runs just enough of the divine image to make us always long for our Creator. We have a connection with God that we seldom acknowledge or celebrate as much as we should.

The Reality of Solitude

We become aware of this divine connection in ways that are predictable and in ways that are filled with mystery. One of the most dramatic ways to become aware of the divine connection is by being alone. The vast majority of our days and nights cover our divine connection with layers of labels and attempts to satisfy our deepest need. Why does the meaning so many of us desire always seem just out of the reach? Once we claim the divine dimension of our existence, we perceive everything differently.

The Genesis story provides a powerful and dramatic image of our basic connection. In the earlier of the two creation stories, God is depicted as stooping over like a potter and shaping the human form out of the clay. The most important part of the image is of God breathing His divine life into the human form. That is our beginning. Somewhere along the way, we have forgotten this basic truth.

No question is closer to the center of our human existence than that of our identity. My question—"Who am I?"—is no different from the question raised by person after person through the ages. Through the years, we seem to have forgotten who we are and where we come from. We will explore this more later. For the moment, I simply say that this sense of being that comes from the Father supercedes everything else in our lives. Understanding life this way does not make other things unimportant. Those things simply take on a different role. We can claim them as gifts, but we should not depend on them. Only the Eternal can truly satisfy.

As I discussed the issue of self-identity with a colleague, he raised a good question: "Do you think that deep within us is a desire to return to Eden?" Whether you determine Eden historically or metaphorically, the question is intriguing. Do we not long for the intimacy of Eden, where there is constant communion with God? Is that not what the Celtic Saints longed for when they prayed and begged for the monastic life? Do we not recognize that beneath all the layers we place on our existence, a sense of being connects us to the Origin of all life? Do we not often long for it and not understand hunger of our souls? Is claiming this sense of being that connects us to God the answer to the need of so many people today? These questions and more form the basis of the journey I am about to share.

Claiming this sense of being, this spark of the Creator God, addresses another question and dilemma of life. When it is all done on this earth for us as individuals, what do we fall back on? When we leave behind what we do and where we live and what we own and to whom we are related, only one thing remains: this sense of life that has been granted us as a child of the Father. At the end of life as we know it here, that is all we have left, and that is all that we need. As Dr. John Claypool has said, "When death comes, we have to trust God, for we have no other option."

If we have never thought of ourselves apart from these external labels, death can be frightening. Once we discover the sense of being beneath all the layers, we lose our biggest reason to be afraid. What we were granted at the moment of our creation will carry us through to the next stage of the journey. We brought that spark of life into the present stage of the journey. That same spark of life and the One who granted it will be the sacred midwife for whatever comes next.

So, you see, this book is not about rhetoric. It is about life that supercedes everything around us. Claiming that life does not make our labels unimportant. Instead, we can then claim them and celebrate them as they were meant to be. They are gifts that pass. None of them last indefinitely. Only one thing remains. It is the life that God gives us and the sense of being to which He calls us. One fact is clear—*being precedes doing*. Life's most important discovery hangs on that fact.

Defined By What We Do

I am among the fortunate people who are privileged to wake up each morning and go to a job that is exactly what they want to do. Since my teen years, being involved in some type of ministry has been the only professional aspiration I have ever known. Because of this mysterious, inner sense of call to ministry, my work is truly what I enjoy.

The down side is that when you combine inner call, profound satisfaction, and long tenure, the result is a too-defining profession. My job so characterizes my self-perception that it becomes difficult to separate myself from what I do professionally. Whenever I introduce myself, I tend to give my name and then almost automatically add that I am a minister. Why? I have many reasons, but the main one is that my self-perception is entirely too dependent upon what I do professionally.

Most of us tend to define each other by what we do. I recently traveled out of the country for several weeks. During that time, I had numerous opportunities to meet people. With rare exception, almost everyone I met asked, "And what do you do for a living?" We all do it. "Hello. What is your name? Where are you from? What do you do there?" With the exception of name and home, our profession becomes one of the primary ways we label each other.

To understand how and why this tendency has developed, we must understand how attitudes toward work have changed through the centuries, especially from the time just prior to the Reformation all the way to our attitudes today. The way culture perceives of work has an interesting history.

Punishment for Original Sin

Work has not always had such a respected reputation. Up to the time of the Reformation, people perceived labor as being forced upon one who was not blessed by God. Work was a part of the curse for sinful humanity. It was not simply a religious issue. For centuries, the elite class looked down on work. The sign of God's blessing was to have work done *for* you, not *by* you.

Discoveries of well-preserved members of the monastic orders in Europe indicate that these individuals were high-ranking priests or bishops. Their hands are the clue because they give little indication of physical labor. Physical labor was beneath the ruling class. They figured God made servants to do the bidding of God's chosen.

Protestant Work Ethic

Then came Martin Luther in the fifteenth century. Luther strongly believed that poverty was not to be desired and was not a divine pronouncement of dissatisfaction. While human beings were in the world to serve God and others, labor was not a curse. The mark of a good person was not the absence of labor but labor used as a way of serving God and others.

Luther developed the unusual and sometimes unwelcomed concept of a worldly calling. This calling was not to be confused with the calling of the monastic life of the Roman Catholic Church. The calling Luther had in mind stood in contrast with the centuries-old concept of work as a curse. According to Luther, one's work was not merely atonement for original sin. It was a way in which to carry out one's service to God.

John Calvin, taking the perception of labor one step further, taught the principle of maximum effort. When a person produces more than is needed, the excess should not be spent on personal appetites. Interestingly, the excess should be reinvested to improve one's work and, therefore, produce greater surpluses for the glory of God. In other words, a person should not selfishly indulge in the excess above what he or she actually needed.

At that point, a major shift occurred in the general attitude toward making profits. The perception prior to this time associated profit making with the role of the oppressor. However, wealth began to be understood as a sign of God's favor and blessing. Not only was working approved, but making a profit was blessed as long as the person used it to the glory of God.

Work that was once understood as atonement was newly perceived as good. But people were to remember to work for the glory of God, since their calling to work came from God. People now proved their worth to themselves and to God by their dedicated labor. All restrictions went by the wayside. Working became a way of demonstrating moral character.

Another interesting by-product emerged within the framework of this new work ethic. A strong emphasis on thrift discouraged workers from spending large amounts of money on personal pleasures. Profits were encouraged as a way of serving and honoring God, but unnecessary luxuries were seen as a distraction from duties to God. The assumption was that God would bless with success anyone dedicated to their work and willing to work hard. As a result, hard-working and thrifty people were considered good and virtuous. This new value of work was a long way from being understood as atonement for sin. Work became a positive value in life. Anyone who was lazy and/or wasteful was not affirmed. The ethic placed great emphasis on personal responsibility.

Although the Protestant Ethic eventually passed from the favor of the masses, remnants of that perception of life and work remain to this day. On the surface, it appears that the attitudes of our current builder generation (World War II generation) reflect much of the Protestant Ethic. While there are similarities, one important factor for the builder generation is the lingering impact of the Great Depression. While their attitudes would embrace many of the same components of the Protestant Ethic, fear and caution play a big role. Memories remain of being unprepared and destitute. Caution, therefore, demands similar attitudes of thrift and an unrelenting willingness to work hard. One guards against excessive living because such a lifestyle would use up what might be needed for another rainy day.

In 1904, German sociologist Max Weber wrote a famous essay, "The Protestant Ethic and the Spirit of Capitalism." He proposed that the principles of the Protestant Ethic contributed to the advancement of the economic system called capitalism. Capitalism maintains that the competition of individuals for wealth through work helps build a strong economy.

Success Became the End

Years later, theologian John Wesley pointed out what he thought would be a negative result of the Protestant Ethic. According to Wesley, there was little question that such an expression of faith would produce industry and frugality, which would in turn produce wealth. Wesley believed that as riches increased, so would the temptation toward pride, anger, and desire. He believed the system would become its own worst enemy and lead to its own downfall. In theory, the Protestant Ethic worked well, but the human dimension would destroy it. Wesley's solution to the dilemma was to encourage people to share their wealth so they would grow in grace.

No country more clearly demonstrated the presence of the Protestant Ethic than early America. At the same time, no country more clearly demonstrated the opposite of John Wesley's wisdom. Wealth did increase in America, and riches became the symbol of respectability. Wesley was right in that wealth became an end in itself rather than a way of glorifying God. It was no longer a means of growing in God's grace but a goal for its own purposes. Material success became the ultimate aspiration. For most people, wealth had little or nothing to do with honoring God. *Wealthy* was the best defining adjective man or woman could hope for.

A sense of spiritual calling dissolved into the industrialized society that developed. Work as personal gain became the motivation for owner and operator. The people wedged into the industrialized environment found little meaning in their work. They rarely felt called by God to do a certain job. The job became simply a way to make a living, often with few if any other options.

For many workers, frustration was the result. They experienced little prestige, and their primary justification, if not the only one, for going in each day was a paycheck. Meaning was not to be found in one's calling to a particular job. Compensation motivated people to work.

Major Shift Toward Consumption

During the twentieth century, a profound change occurred in the perception of work and profession, reaching its peak late as the century came to a close. The Protestant Ethic shifted to a consumer ethic. The difference between the two is significant. In the Protestant Ethic people were encouraged to work hard and save money. The basic philosophy of the consumption ethic, or consumerism, is to work as little as possible and spend the money as soon as possible since it will not be worth as much tomorrow. The focus of the Protestant Ethic is the future. The consumption ethic places more importance on the present, often at the expense of the future.

In most cases, honoring God with one's labor gave way to the need to have all the things money can buy. The collection of things became people's driving force. As the bumper sticker said, "The man who dies with the most toys wins."

An Unexpected Shift

The path of consumerism has taken a surprising turn. Instead of work becoming less important since its inherent meaning has been reduced, work has taken on new importance. The importance is not a result of honoring God with one's profession or of the inherent meaning found in working. Its value comes from the importance of the things one's labor can produce. The desire to consume makes workers obsessed with the labor that will ultimately provide it.

Our insecurities force us to work harder and harder to provide the things we believe will ultimately provide the meaning we seek. Our consumption ties us closer and closer to our professions. We work hard not to honor God's calling or to share with the less fortunate.

Instead, consumerism demands more from us, and the way we play the game is to work harder and make even more money to spend.

If our value is secured by our work, the temptation is to produce more to increase our worth. What appears to be adding to our net worth becomes an effort to add to our personal value as human beings. A logical spin-off is that we push ourselves beyond normal limits in an effort to feel better about ourselves.

We become identified with our work because it seems to be the best way to secure the meaning we seek in "things." Is this issue not at the heart of so much struggle and frustration today? Many people have worked hard. They have acquired many things. Yet, when they assess what they have acquired, it does not seem to add up to the meaning they anticipated. Many people look around their possessions and ask, "Is this what I have struggled for?" Surely there is more to life than this!

Never Enough

The biggest weakness in today's consumption ethic is that we can never buy enough to provide meaning for our lives. There is always something bigger than what we have. There is always more to acquire. We cling to our profession and our desire to buy because we always see someone who can out-buy us. If we let go and relax, we may lose our status symbols and our self-induced status-conscious ladder of success.

If in the Protestant Ethic we proved our worth to *God* by what we produced, in today's ethic we prove ourselves to *ourselves*, or so we think, by what we produce and by what we are able to consume. Somewhere along the way we have begun to measure ourselves by productivity and its resulting consumption. It has little or nothing to do with honoring God. It has everything to do with measuring our worth to ourselves.

Once our worth is determined by productivity and consumption, we are set up for major problems. It is merely a question of time. For example, from where does our worth come if disability prevents physical labor? Or where is our value when retirement comes by choice or force? What happens to our worth when, unrelated to our performance, displacement occurs? The circumstances of loss may be out of our control, but being unemployed feels the same.

The Inevitable Result

If our sense of being depends on our profession and/or the ability to provide all the things that consumerism demands, then what lies beneath that role? Who are we when we no longer have a business card to define us? Our labor can have enormous value for us. It can, as Luther described, be a response to God's call, even in the business world. And we can certainly find in our labors a way to honor God. Peel off the layer of "what we do for a living," though, and what is underneath? Going through life with only a professional identity is risky business. We are much safer when we value our lives on a more permanent and predictable measure.

Our value cannot come from what we accumulate around us. He who dies with the most toys does not win. He still dies! Our worth has to come from the One in whose image we are created. The divine spark and sense of being we inherit from the Creator is a much more dependable basis on which to value our lives. Holy Scripture describes Jesus as having a "name above every name" (Phil 2:9). Our name may not be above every name, but it is, indeed, a name! Our value comes not from our business card or from the number of things we accumulate, but from the One who created us and lives within us.

Chapter 2

Being:
The Source

"So, I have come down . . . ."—Exodus 3:8b

If God calls us "to be," then from where does that sense of being come? What is the source and origin? Does it originate in us? Do we obtain it by merely the experience of our birth? Is it conferred upon us at some stage of our existence, possibly a certain age? Does it come to us after we go through a certain number of life experiences? Is it the compensation we receive for the loss of our innocence?

There is no way to begin the process of answering that question without going back to the description of our human creation. Genesis 1:27 says, "So God created man in his own image, in the image of God he created him; male and female he created them." If, then, we are created in God's image and have within us a small spark of the divine, there must be a connection with the way we experience being and the way God acknowledges that property in Himself. In other words, what it means for us *to be* is related to the way God experiences His own sense of *being*. At the risk of repetition, if we believe that we are created in the image of God, born with a spark of the divine, then somehow our sense of being must be related to God, in one way or another coming from Him.

The earliest biblical glimpses of God's divine nature are found in Genesis 2 and Exodus 3. I have already referred to the creation account and its unquestionable role in understanding who we are. To add to that picture, there is no better Scripture for explaining what *being* means to God than the Exodus account. Chapter 3 contains the well-known story of Moses encountering God at the burning bush. Moses was tending the flock of his father-in-law as he came to Mount Horeb. There he encountered the burning bush and an angel, both of which got his attention. This famous encounter is far too complex to sum up in a few sentences. Yet, we must give attention to two specific images—points that offer a small ray of revelation about the nature of God.

Two Images of Self-disclosure

The first image is from Exodus 3:8 and the phrase "I have come down . . . ." These are the words of a God who does not sit privately in the heavens, lost in Himself, nor does He exist in blindness of the human experience. That simple phrase frames the character of a God who moves into history with a longing to connect to those created in His image. When God connects with us, we receive an image about life. Too often, however, we dismiss the events as coincidental. We can never separate God and history. Instead, God is always in history. This simple phrase from Exodus gives a clue about that.

The second image comes from the dialogue between Moses and God. It is an exchange so familiar that we might overlook one of the most important definitions of who God is. This window of light about God comes from the simple conversation about God's name. Moses was instructed to go back to Egypt. To do so, he would need to tell the people who sent him. In whose name would he go to Pharaoh? He was told to say, "The God of your fathers has sent me to you."

That was not enough for Moses. There were many gods in the culture of that day, and Moses needed to identify the specific one who sent him. Yet, when God identifies Himself as "I Am Who I Am," He does much more than make a play on words. Next to the revelation of Himself in our Lord Jesus, this phrase is one of the most important self-disclosures God ever makes in the Bible.

God's Disclosure

In the mere act of giving His name, God shares so much about Himself, even if the name sounds strange to our ears. In ancient Israel, a person's name was the summation of his or her character. On the other hand, the refusal to share one's name was understood as a clear intention of the person's unwillingness to disclose himself or herself completely to another. Knowing another person's name implied the granting of some degree of power or control over the person whose name was revealed. Hence, it is important to note that God willingly reveals His personal name to Moses. At least, God cracks the window a bit and allows a narrow measure of light concerning His mysterious nature. Even if not full disclosure, God obviously declares Himself to Moses, revealing that God desires to be known.

God reveals His own sense of being when He responds by saying, "This is what you are to say to the Israelites: 'I Am has sent you.'" On one level the statement seems vague, as if conveying more than is actually stated. It certainly does not give full disclosure. Even with this historical revelation, there remains the hiddenness of God, grounded in His incomparable nature. When God speaks of being, He is not talking philosophically, but His revelation is that of an active being. His "I am that I am" is not merely an ideological concept, but a summation of all God is. This divine name, now revealed to Moses, was a summing up of the divine character and attributes of God.

Beyond the Present Moment

Old Testament scholars agree that the phrase can also be understood as "I Will Be Who I Will Be." Therefore, it underscores the continuing revelation of God. The word "final" is never part of God's self-disclosure. There will always be a continual unfolding of who God is. We cannot capture with precision the full nature of God at any point in time; we must allow for the possibility of continuing insight.

All we will ever know about God is what God chooses to let us know. It will always be a partial understanding. Yet, let it be clear that God first describes Himself to us by pointing to His being—"I am." John Durham in *The Exodus Biblical Commentary* has an interesting description of God's statement of self-revelation: "It is a reply that suggests that it is inappropriate to refer to God as 'was' or 'will be,' for the reality of this active existence can be suggested only by the present: 'is' or 'is-ing,' 'Always Is,' or 'Am.'"[1]

The title God chose to designate Himself to Moses is more than just a title. It directly expresses the quality of God's being. However, it is not *being* as an abstract, philosophical notion, but *being* in the sense of the reality of God's active, dynamic presence. As the writer of the *Broadman Commentary* describes, "Although continually present as a God who does not change, he is at the same time present in every generation with new connotations and implications."[2]

When God referred to Himself as "I am" or "I will be," it was the total of all His divine character. He was claiming all that He was to Himself and to humankind. We should not get so caught up in God's unusual rendering of a name that we overlook one of the most important insights into the divine nature of God and into human nature. For God, being precedes doing. Before we can understand what God does, we must understand who He is. Who is He? "He is!" Nahum Sarna, in his book *Exploring Exodus*, writes, "Whether it means 'I Am That I Am,' or 'I Am Who I Am,' or 'I Will Be Who I Will Be'—and it can mean any of these—God's pronouncement of His own name indicates that the Divine Personality can be known only to the extent that God chooses to reveal Himself, and it can be truly characterized only in terms of itself, and not by analogy with something else."[3]

Exodus 3 gives us a powerful revelation. What is shared about God's divine nature is only a glimpse. Yet, if we are created, as Scripture describes, in the image of God, then in some way our own sense of being is reflected in God's revealing of Himself. If we are a speck of God's image, Exodus 3 is important to us. In this picture, we find an image of ourselves. Gunnar Tidestrom adds an additional thought to this revealing description: "It is strange that, though we all say our 'I am,' we nevertheless fancy ourselves to be so far, so essentially, separated from one another. Is not the same spirit in all of us which from our thousand mouths says his 'I am,' thus proving himself and us true?"[4]

Our sense of being does not come from circumstances or experiences. It is a unique core of life within each one of us that comes from the Creator Himself. It is the gift of living that is deep within our souls. It is from that spark of the Creator's image within us that is at the heart of our need to be. There is obviously uniqueness in God's being. Since we are created in God's image and within us is a spark of the divine, there is uniqueness in our existence as well. While we are not self-sustaining as God is, we are unique and are not dependent upon anyone else to give us the right of existence. Much of our sadness is the result of granting other people and other realities the undeserved role of affirming our existence. Our connection comes from one source, the ultimate Source of life and identity.

A Important Point to Ponder

An additional point deserves to be raised. It has to do with our worship of God and how His disclosure of Himself should influence our praise. If we are honest, we will confess that most of our praise of God relates to what God does. While we should never undervalue the active presence of God in our lives, we should not limit our praise of Him only in response to what He does. Do we forget to praise Him for Who He is?

In several small groups I did an informal survey by asking people to share with me their definitions of God. I asked them to write their definitions, hoping they would be more honest. Most of their definitions described God in terms of what He does. With rare exception did anyone refer to God in terms of His being. Our natural tendency is to think of God in terms of what He does for us. Yet one of the first titles God gives to Himself relates to His being—"*I am.*"

When God identified himself based on the Hebrew verb "to be," He set Himself apart from the loosely related tribal existence of God to a specific God who above all else existed independently of all things. Knowing that about God, should we not still praise Him for being that God? Yes, of course, we should praise God for what He does. On the other hand, knowing what we know about Him from His own self-disclosure, we should praise Him first and foremost just for being God. Do we remember to do that, to begin there? The temptation is great to skip to what God does or what we suggest He should do in the future. But "I am" is how God first desired to be known. Would God desire otherwise even now? One fact of life is always assured—the fact of God's presence and the fact that "God is." Just as importantly, His being precedes His doing.

Notes

[1] John Durham, "Exodus," *Exodus Biblical Commentary* (Nashville: Broadman Holman, 2000), 334.

[2] Roy Honeycutt, "Exodus," *Broadman Commentary* (Nashville: Broadman, 1969), 332.

[3] Nahum Sarna, *Exploring Exodus: The Heritage of Biblical Israel* (New York: Schocken Books, 1986), 43.

[4] Gunnar Tidestrom, *Runeberg* (Helsingfors: Mercators Tryckeri, 1941), 395.

Chapter 3

Being:
A Time of Discovery

"Be still and know that I am God . . . ." —Psalm 46

For a long time I have struggled with what sounds like a rhetorical or philosophical question: "Who are we?" From a personal perspective, it's "Who am I?" More specifically, "Who am I underneath all the labels that define me?" Ask me who I am and I will tell you my age, what I do for a living, and something about my family. These labels are all well and good, but is there not more to me than these external labels?

Because of my tenure in my pastorate, I recently became eligible for a brief sabbatical. Having time to spend is an exciting experience. As I began to plan, I hoped I might be able to use this sabbatical time to address my need to get my mind around what it means for me to *be*. My first inclination was to spend a month in a monastery. I reasoned that in a monastery I would be separated from many of the things that daily define me.

I assumed these monastic circumstances would dramatically cut me off from my normal routine. This kind of setting would become a laboratory for getting in touch with a piece of me that is covered by so many other layers of life. However, what first seemed like a good idea eventually became an uninviting way to spend a few weeks away from the normal routine. The more I thought about it, the more the setting of a monastery seemed grey and cold. After all, it would be fall or winter at that time. So I just let the idea fade away and made no final plans for anything definite.

Then, as a result of a conversation with a colleague, I learned of a small church on an island in Scotland that might be a possibility for a visit. A colleague had recently been there and described it as beautiful and isolated. Maybe I could offer myself to the church on the island. Surely I had something that might be of value to them. In return, when not involved with them, I would be alone and have my imagined experience with solitude. Maybe in this setting, like in a monastery, I would be forced to deal with personal issues precisely because there would be nothing else to do. As it turned out, it worked out that way. Truthfully, I could do little for the church. Some teaching and preaching required very little time. The rest of the time became a laboratory for being alone, isolated from most of my usual definitions of myself.

A Gift Emerges for Me

Instead of my original plan of staying in a monastery room, surrounded by grey walls, I found myself in a small but quaint attic room in a hostel overlooking the village and ocean. That room would become a solitary place for me over the next few weeks. It would become a place to which I would ache to return in the following months.

For several consecutive days, I had no interaction with anyone from the church. I spent hours upon hours in my room, reading, praying, and writing. There was no phone and no one knocking on my door. I had no obligations and no responsibilities. There was no schedule to keep. I could read, write, and sleep, and no one knew and no one cared. The most dramatic difference was that all the things that normally directed my waking hours were suddenly gone, and I found myself experiencing, maybe for the first time in my life, true solitude.

I remember my first day of such solitude. I actually slept late, though I did not mean to. I suppose I was just tired and my body needed it. I awakened with none of the usual stimuli that normally direct my day. One thought was that I could get ahead with sermon writing. The minister of music, my colleague at church, would appreciate that kind of prior planning. After considering that noble concern, I instead picked up a book and began reading. Why? It was lying on the table, and reading it seemed like a good thing to do. I read a lot in my professional life, usually because the book or article relates to something I am producing. This day was different. I simply read because the book was there.

I remembered that I had not gone through any of my normal devotional routine. So I read from my devotional book, but I did not hurry as I often do. In fact, I went back and read past devotionals I had missed. Why? Because the book was there. Then, still sitting in my chair in this small, pleasant room, I began looking through upcoming Lectionary readings. Why? Because copies of the Lectionary readings happened to be on the table in front of me. I sat in my chair for hours reading exactly what I wanted to read. I even fell asleep once or twice for brief periods of time. No one knew and no one cared how I spent my time.

More Difficult Than Imagined

In spite of the change of routine, that first day was difficult for me. All the things that normally directed my time and consumed my energy were not present that day, and it became my first experience with true solitude. I made intriguing discoveries that first day that were profound and enlightening for me.

For example, I had anticipated that solitude would offer a bit of a challenge. The truth is that at first it was more difficult than I expected. In fact, I became quite anxious, almost panicked, during that first day. I knew my wife would not join me for several more weeks. The little church would have no more demands tomorrow than they did today. I began to question if I could make it through this experience. That description may sound a bit dramatic, but it was the truth.

Talking about solitude comes easily. Most of us know solitude probably holds inherent value. I have preached and taught about its benefits. In Scotland, I discovered that solitude is an experience far more powerful than I ever expected. I found myself surrounded by silence. It was new territory, a brand-new land.

I realized that I must learn to navigate by a completely different set of signs. Most of the external signposts on which I had depended for so long were not present. I had to find another way of determining my thoughts and actions. It is one thing to talk about silence and solitude. It is another thing to genuinely experience it over a long period of time. Be careful in assuming yourself to be an expert just because you have read a good book on solitude or have on occasion been alone for a few hours!

God in the World and God within Me

I believe God is active in the world. He is busy in redemptive work and constantly invites us to join Him in the world. Whenever we think we have initiated a work for God in the world, we usually discover that He has long already been there, inviting us to join Him. God in the world as an active presence is a safe assumption. My ministry has rested on that assumption for many years.

However, I have not fully given myself to actively, genuinely seeking God *within me*. I have come to believe that God waits in the depths of our being to speak to us if we are still long enough to hear His voice. The hearing of that voice comes in many ways. Seldom is it an audible voice that speaks in the King's English. For me, the voice comes in a whisper.

I had assumed that being still and listening would not come easy, and it didn't. As I became still, I did not fully experience the silence at first. In fact, I heard many voices. I was not hallucinating or experiencing any illness. In silence, perceived voices emerge. Most of them were voices of the routine apprehensions that are a part of my life. Some related to work, to family, and to other dimensions of life from which one does not simply immediately disconnect.

These were moments of unrest. I was determined to pay attention to the unrest but not be ruled by it. Yet, I repeated silently to myself the well-known tenth verse of Psalm 46: "Be still and know that I am God." I was determined to follow through with my solitude and make friends with silence. There finally came a time when the voices of unrest gave way to a hushed whisper. I don't know that this was a totally new place for me. I can say that I had not visited it often. It was on that day more than any other time in my life that I could truly appreciate the psalmist's words, "Be still and know." In the silence of that first day, I truly understood the meaning of hearing the still small voice. I have heard it before, but never more profoundly than on that day.

Willing to Wait

I believe my most important discovery came in realizing the importance of waiting. I have been still before. I am not a newcomer to a devotional life. However, most of the time I make a quick attempt to enter into silence, yet it must fit my schedule. The problem for me has not been in scheduling it, but in providing enough time for something of value to take place. One may be able to schedule solitude, but truly experiencing it is another thing.

A scheduled and timed devotional life is better than none at all. Even better, however, are times when the alarm clock is not set to end the solitude just as it begins. In Scotland, waiting became a key for me. God may or may not follow our rigid schedule. To often, we schedule God in our lives like we schedule reading the morning newspaper. Ten minutes before or after breakfast may not best capture God's presence and plan for that day. The struggle with waiting is important enough to warrant separate and specific treatment in later pages of this book.

Becoming Responsible

It seems that an important part of the discovery of being is the willingness to become vulnerable and responsible. We convince ourselves that our hurried lives are basically altruistic. In other words, most of us like to think we are meeting the needs of other people around us for their sake alone. Truthfully, we often use commitments and demands as a way of taking us off the hook. By handing over the way I organize my life to other needs, I am relieved of choosing the best use of a given period of time. The solitude I experienced on Westray Island forced me to be honest about why I stay so busy.

All the things that normally drive me were stripped away in my solitude. I learned that it is much easier to hand over how I use my day to the claims and demands of other people than to be accountable to myself as to how I spend my waking hours. Suddenly, no one was telling me how to spend my time, and that became more profound when I realized that tomorrow would be the same.

As challenging as the solitude was, I anticipated some of the struggle. One dimension of solitude that caught me by surprise was the silence. In a world polluted by noise, how could silence possibly be intimidating? Like solitude, silence becomes an easy subject for advice and discussion. When one is surrounded by it, though, it takes on different meaning.

The setting provided so much opportunity for silence. The island itself is a quiet place. Only 575 quiet people inhabit it. The people of Westray are beautiful, and one of their enviable qualities is that they never shout. They simply don't raise their voices. It is a part of their culture. Those periodically walking by the hostel seemed to pass with hushed tones. Occasionally, a car would pass by on the single-lane road in front, and the wind would come over the water against the window. Yet, generally speaking, I heard none of the sounds I am accustomed to hearing. I became consumed by the silence and really didn't know what to do with it. I became aware of even the smallest noises.

Nothing interrupted my reading and meditation except my own mental wanderings. One silly example of how conscious I became of silence was when I took a piece of gum from my pocket. After a few seconds of chewing, I decided to spit it out. Chewing it made too much noise. Have you ever noticed how much noise you make when you chew a piece of gum? Probably not. I can honestly tell you that I never confronted that issue before my experience in Westray. Yet, when you become so aware of silence, you don't want anything to interrupt it. The silence becomes sacred time and sacred space. One day as I worked, I remembered lines from a devotional book from which I had read earlier that same day:

> Come with me by yourselves and rest awhile,
> I know you're weary of the stress and throng,
> Wipe from your brow the sweat and dust of toil,
> and in My quiet strength again be strong.
>
> Come now aside from all the world holds dear,
> For fellowship the world has never known,
> Alone with me, and with My Father here,
> With Me and with My Father, not alone.
>
> Then from fellowship with your Lord return,
> And work till daylight softens into even:
> Those brief hours are not lost in which you learn
> More of your Master and His rest in Heaven.[1]

What made solitude and silence such a challenge for me in those initial hours was that with all the external stimuli taken away from me, I had to direct my use of the day, my thoughts, and my actions based on stimuli from within instead of without. It is easier to let someone else or a current task make those decisions for me.

Decisions Must Come from Within

My Scotland experience may sound overstated, but it was a profound discovery for me. Another enlightening part of the experience is that I found this space of silence to be tiring through that first day. It required more from me than I expected. The solitude and silence did not become an escape from myself. The truth is that I could not escape myself. Self-awareness took on new meaning for me, and I came closer that day than ever before to what it means "to be." Being became a reality for me when the things that normally dictate my life were peeled away. I had only myself and a strong sense of God's presence to confront, which was both energizing and frightening. My experiences of solitude did not end with that day's experience.

I thought of what I had read of the early saints. So many of them discovered the necessity of solitude. One early church father named Patrick acknowledged that he would turn to God in as many as a hundred prayers a day. Patrick discovered in his solitude that he was never alone. He learned that God was always with him. God's power would always be present.

I am convinced from my own experience that another issue we face in solitude is vulnerability before God. I felt exposed before God. In my normal daily routine, I can construct enough interruption and busyness to prevent my being too vulnerable. If I feel God is getting too close, I can hurry out to do His work. After all, God should be pleased with my busyness for His sake. Shouldn't He? Or could it be that He would rather have my full attention at times when my heart and head become open for inspection?

In those quiet, silent moments, we discover one of the most important lessons in life. Specifically, God is not a theory to be analyzed or a subject to be studied. Too many of us approach God as a problem to be solved. Instead, God is a presence and a relationship offered to us for living and enjoying. As we encounter God, we come to terms with the fact that if our minds are too small to grasp the presence of God, our hearts are big enough to accept Him.

Moses Reconsidered

We talked in chapter 2 about Moses' historic encounter with God. We briefly considered what this encounter teaches us about God, but we failed to point out what this encounter teaches us about Moses. Do you not find it interesting that God waited until this particular moment to confront Moses with His plan for the future? There must have been many critical moments in Egypt when God could have given Moses an outline for the liberation of the Israelites. Yet, do not ignore the time God selected. God chose the time when Moses was alone and quiet in the desert. At that moment, Moses was stripped of all his influence and prestige. Moses was alone with himself, so he thought, in the quiet of the desert. There were no interruptions and few demands. Then, out of nowhere Moses encountered a bush that was on fire but not consumed.

This desert encounter is a classic experience to remember. For the first few moments, Moses raised a question about the nature of the burning bush. However, Moses quickly shifted his attention from the ways God was expressing Himself to the actual One who initiated the encounter. The sacred presence of God totally consumed Moses.

This experience is replayed in our own encounters. Have you been on a mountainside in solitude? At first you focus on the surroundings. How can you not notice? But once you begin to commune with the living presence of the Holy One, the surroundings become secondary. In solitude, the silence and the surroundings become a medium through which God captures your total attention. Like Moses, we too forget about the burning bush. Like Moses, we become totally immersed in the presence of the Holy One.

The Need for Solitude

The truth is that we periodically need solitude and silence in order to have a better sense of what it means to be. In hearing God's still voice, we are able to get in touch with the spark of being we inherit from the Father. Most of the time, we keep that sacred spark covered by all the other things that define us.

Steve Langford, pastor of the Baptist Church of Westray, Scotland, describes the silent moments of prayer in the following way:

> I once heard the journey of prayer time described as being like descending from the surface of the sea to the depths of the ocean in a kind of diving chamber. The turbulent waves on the surface represent the agitated surface of the mind as we respond to everyday pressures. As you begin to be still and patiently attend to the silence, which like a diving chamber is taking you slowly down, you begin to leave the immediate world of agitated thought behind.
>
> But, as you descend everything below the surface is by no means calm. Some distance down there are to be found the huge currents of the ocean. These correspond to the powerful psychological forces that run below the surface of our minds and, often unknown to us, drive and shape what we do and how we behave. Here can be found our need to succeed, our addiction to work, our fear of emptiness, our craving for recognition, our fear of failure—powerful forces that drive us on and make us the people we often wish we were not.
>
> In the silence of our prayer, with our minds starved of distractions, we may become freshly and disconcertingly aware of them. However, our persistent faithfulness and attention to the Word and to the Lord's presence will take us deeper and away from these distractions. Eventually we arrive at the bottom of the ocean to a place where the currents have finally ceased altogether and where it is utterly silent and dark and still. Here there is no movement at all. Here it is possible to rest with a great sense of gratitude. Here God dwells, and in secret, you dwell in Him. [shared by permission]

Elijah Discovered It

Do you remember the story of Elijah? For whatever reason, after Elijah had conveyed the news to Ahab that there would be no rain in the next few years, God ordered Elijah to go to the Kerith Ravine. Elijah was told to go there and hide. The ravens would feed him. It was a strange plan, but that was the way it would be for Elijah. It seems fairly obvious that if he would be drinking from the brook there and depending on the ravens for food, Elijah would be placing his dependency upon God. Is that not one of the expectations of solitude? By the act of one becoming more conscious of God's presence, is not a sense of dependency an expected outcome?

Solitude places us in what has been termed the hidden side of life. In a culture where we often measure our value by how well we are known and how much others depend on us, is there not great value in God sending us to a Kerith Ravine? Our Kerith Ravine is occasionally forced upon us by sickness, disability, or sorrow. Yet, the most valuable experiences of our Kerith Ravine are those when we willingly, even voluntarily, hide from normal things and from other people, hiding from all except the Creator God. As a result, we put ourselves into a position to be able to say with all honesty, "I desire nothing but your will. Reveal it to me."

The story is told that Lancelot Andrews, a seventeenth century bishop, spent five hours of every day in prayer and devotion to God. Many of the Celtic saints spent the majority of their waking hours in prayer and meditation. Author David Adam refers to it as "walking the edges."[2]

Jesus experienced His Kerith Ravine in many places. He "walked the edges" as He sought the wilderness, the Garden of Gethsemane, and the solitude of other solitary places. Those precious hours were not punishment for anything. They provided the direction and energy He needed to face the challenging hours ahead. God's best servants must understand the value of the hidden side of life.

From Instinct to Principle

Another value of the hidden life, a life that practices solitude, is that it allows one to move from operating on mere instinct to developing deep-seated principles on which to base one's actions. When one is seldom alone with God, there is little opportunity to understand God's will for one's life. When one has even a marginal understanding of God's will, life can be approached with a better sense of purpose and a desire to be faithful.

When we do not provide those hidden moments for ourselves, we are left to make important life decisions based only on instinct and impulse. The wisdom and strength we gain in solitude allows us to move through sorrow and storms with greater power and direction. The reason is clear. We are finally able to act and commit from within instead of depending totally on external factors.

Notes

[1] L. B. Cowman, *Streams in the Desert* (Grand Rapids MI: Zondervan, 1997), 372.

[2] David Adam, *Walking the Edges* (London: Holy Trinity Church: Society for Promoting Christian Knowledge, 2003), 54.

Chapter 4

Being:
Discovering and
Sharing Our Best Gift

The Word became flesh and made his dwelling among us. —John 1:14a

Checking my calendar, I realized that I needed to be in Greenville, South Carolina, on Friday of that week. I had a meeting at Furman University, my alma mater. The President's Advisory Council would begin promptly at 8:00 AM. Greenville is a two-hour drive from my hometown, so I knew I must either get up early or drive over the night before. In an effort to avoid the unknown of early morning travel, I decided that driving over the night before would be a better idea.

All that sounds good, but I am not being totally transparent. The truth is that our son and his family live in Greenville, and I was not nearly as concerned to be on time for the meeting as I was to spend the night with them. You see, they happen to be the parents of the world's most beautiful granddaughter. If we have other grandchildren, I will feel the same way about them. However, right now Ashlyn is the only grandchild and therefore has that sole honor all to herself.

Thinking through my plan a little more, I realized that if I could get away from my office before "quitting time" on Thursday, I could arrive at their house for a late dinner and maybe even time to go out for ice cream. It was the best choice to make sure I was not late for the Friday morning meeting. I was all heart for Furman. Right? The sacrifices we make!

My plan worked perfectly. I got away just ahead of the traffic on Thursday. By 6:30 PM I was eating a grilled hamburger with Ashlyn. Oh yes, Chris and Heather were there too, I think. When I suggested ice cream, Ashlyn, who is only two, spoke in perfect, complete sentences that she fully agreed. If Mom and Dad were good, we might let them tag along. After all, ice cream is something grandfather and granddaughter must do together. It is a sacred ritual.

And so we did. We went to the Marble Slab. This is not your average drugstore soda shop. They have ice cream dishes that cost more than my normal lunch allowance. But who was keeping an account? This is a sacred ritual, and you cannot put a price tag on tradition. Ashlyn ate most of her ice cream and some of mine and expressed interest in the selections of several people seated around us. And who was worried about sugar? If she couldn't sleep when we got home, that simply left more time for us to play.

When we returned to the house, everyone was a bit tired. We quickly wiped off the ice cream residue, and Ashlyn climbed into my lap. Thus began the absolute best part of the day, maybe the best part of my year! With her blanket and stuffed dog, she sat in my lap and we rocked. She did not say anything, nor did I. Nothing needed to be said. We just sat together and rocked.

I felt guilty when I prayed that she would not go to sleep too soon. They might put her to bed. With all the sugar she had eaten, the chance of quick sleep was slim. It was a sacred moment. She simply sat in my lap, and one of God's special gifts to me that day was that we sat there together for quite a long time. We did not do anything. We did not talk. It was a simple but wonderful time of being together. It was just *being*.

A Renewed Appreciation

As with most grandparents, my experiences with my grandchild become bigger than life. I will not go so far as to say I never appreciated the value of just being with someone before Ashlyn came along. Obviously there have been many special moments of just being with my loved ones. Yet there is such a renewed appreciation of just being with someone when a grandchild appears.

There are certainly many things I want to do with her, but most of all I just want to be with her. Place, time, or circumstance have nothing to do with it. Those conditions can only add to the experience. It is all about sharing time and space. It is not about doing. It is about being together. I am grateful to God and to Ashlyn for teaching me the value of shared time and space. All too often we are oblivious to those moments.

Gift to Family and Others

Once we begin to claim a sense of being that is not defined by what we do or where we live or what we own, we can then learn the joy of offering to others the best gift we have, the gift of ourselves. For those of us who are married, is this not the gift our spouse would genuinely value from us? And is it not the gift we so often fail to offer? What about our children? As much as they enjoy doing things with us, do they not crave the gift we most often forget to share? For some of us, our grandchildren become our best teachers of the value of being together. Why do we wait so late to learn that lesson?

As adults we frequently worry about whether proper values are finding their lodging in the lives of young boys and girls. How are those values passed on? Are they found in providing the best of everything for our children? Are they found by providing for their financial security? Are values passed on by making sure our children attend positive functions, such as Sunday school or Scouts? Do values come about by the discipline of athletics? Of course, all of these experiences are valuable to the development of our children. The most important way, the most reliable way for values to be passed on to our children, is found in moments of being together. By being, I mean more than just sitting briefly in the same room.

Values are best passed along when our children have quality time to see through the layers of labels and glimpse what is within and underneath. The values our children most need are not from the labels of professional and domestic roles. They long to see what is inside, what motivates us, how we feel about life, and what we know about life.

A Predictable Result

There are many potential losses when family members fail to be together. They may spend time together, but it is so focused on doing things that sharing common time and space seldom becomes an option. The result is increasing unfamiliarity. To state it another way, family members become strangers to each other. I think you would be surprised, possibly amazed, at how little most families know about each other. The reason is clear. Familiarity comes from being together. Intimate knowledge that we assume to be a part of family dynamics is never automatic.

Listen to this Confession

Wes Bigler is the president of the Financial Network in Atlanta. In a recent article in his company's newsletter, he describes the painful experience of his son's sudden and unexpected death. Wes's son, Clint, was shot and killed when four men broke into his apartment in an apparent robbery attempt. He describes with painful honesty how he, like any other parent, would easily trade places if only that were possible. Needless to say, such an exchange is not possible. He also describes how the event of Clint's death has given new meaning to the importance of priorities in life. Allow me to pass on the final paragraph of Wes's article:

It's my sincere wish that my son's death will help you take care of your priorities today. My resolution is that I'm going to do more "being." Why do we feel the need to "do" so much? Why can't we just "be" more? I have been a doer all my life but I believe we need a balance between doing and being. Let's just sit and watch our kids, friends, and families just living. Let's take snapshots of them with our minds and eyes. Our 21st century world is a fast-paced, high-tech life of instant-everything jammed into a 24/7 existence. We are always on the go to another meeting, ball game, piano practice, church function, or dinner party. If I could have one more day with Clint, I would want to just "be" with my son. Stop and spend time with people you love. Stop and spend time with yourself. Take time to sit down in silence and contemplate our world and the blessings we have been given. (used by permission)

Our Best Gift

What is the best gift we can offer a friend in time of loss? During the time of my sabbatical on Westray Island, one of my best friends, a ministry partner in our church, lost his daughter due to the sudden onset of a chronic illness. It was totally unexpected. I cannot imagine the depth of pain for him and his family. The news came to me in a place far away. To get back to Charlotte on time, I would require a perfect series of airline connections over several days. Getting back within the needed time was simply not possible. The reality of not being able to take the place expected of me was one of the most gut-wrenching experiences of my ministry. I am aware that my presence would not have changed the horrible face of reality. The personal struggle for me was that I could not do the one thing I could offer—just be there. There are times when the absolute, only thing we can do for a friend is just be there, show up.

Similar events happen in the lives of every one of us. We can do nothing to turn back the hands of time and change death back to life. We have no magical powers that dramatically change reality. The best gift we offer someone who faces moments that strip meaning from their existence is the gift of our being with them. That does not mean we "camp out" with them or give them the feeling that now they become our caretakers. Rather, it is offering them the gift of presence. Being not only precedes doing. There are times when it stands alone because there is no doing.

Do you remember what Jesus said about salt and light in the Sermon on the Mount? "You are the salt of the earth . . ." (Matt 5:13). "You are the light of the world . . ." (Matt 5:14). He was trying to get across one of the most valuable lessons of life. We have within us the inherent ability to be salt and light. Granted, Jesus was talking to people who had already made a marginal commitment to Him. Yet, within them and within us there is the present ability to be salt and light. He did not give a long list of requirements to accomplish before we could claim saltness and lightness. It is being who we are where and when we are. We are salt and light now. The question before us is whether we are willing to claim our value of being salt and light.

Our Best Example

We should learn this principle from the best teacher of all. Look at what God chose to do when we found ourselves in the midst of a problem we could not fix. Never let it be said that God did not do anything; instead, consider what He did. The way He chose to resolve the problem we created was "to be" with us. There must have been other options available to Him. Yet, He decided to join us in our circumstances and resolve the problem from within. Do not ignore the obvious fact that before He chose to do, He chose to be.

Time and time again we will find ourselves with people who have huge needs. It would be immoral for us to ignore opportunities to do something that would improve their circumstances. Being can never be a cop-out for doing. However, in our haste to do something we often overlook the most important gift we can offer, ourselves. There are times, in fact, when all we can do is give ourselves. It will always be our best gift. Consider how fortunate we are that God chose to be before He decided to do. Otherwise, we would still be in the same mess we got ourselves into. "The Word became flesh and dwelt among us."

Chapter 5

Being: The Discipline of Waiting

. . . the spirit of Jesus would not allow them to go. —Acts 16:7b

Seldom is there a time when "being" stands more in contrast to "doing" than when we are forced into the discipline of waiting. For the majority of us, waiting is in the top-ten list of the most challenging disciplines. Rare is the person who truly enjoys waiting. In the minds of most of us, waiting equals loss of time. It is life placed on hold. That is the case with the small, relatively insignificant experiences of waiting, those times when you are in the checkout line and the person in front of you debates the price of every item. Life on hold seems to describe those times when you are stuck in traffic because some unfortunate soul up ahead has rear-ended another car. It is waiting in line at the DMV office when everyone in the county decides to take care of business the same day you need to change your auto title.

Waiting can also include considerably more life-changing experiences. For some, an illness forces inactivity and waiting. For others, it might be the endless wait when you are looking for a job and family resources are stretched thin. It occurs when you struggle for a promotion and for some reason it never seems to happen. Whether you are waiting for the repair service to finally arrive or whether life is on hold due to a serious illness, waiting can be a challenging time. Life on hold can also be a serious issue of faith. We must remind ourselves that times of waiting are not indications of God's absence. Often they can become moments of learning and strength and clear indicators of God's presence.

The Change of Perception

The first hurdle we must jump is to move away from the perception of waiting as a totally passive experience. Waiting is not unlike the task of active listening. We can listen with a passive ear, or we can listen actively, fully engaging ourselves in what we hear. There is a huge difference between passive and active listening. The same comparison can be made of what often seems to be life on hold, in other words, waiting.

An interesting story in Acts 16 may demonstrate how waiting is often God's way of drawing close and preparing us for the work He has given us. It can become God's way of dramatically redirecting our paths. In this story, Timothy has just joined Paul and Silas. Paul is wired up and fired up to go. The text indicates that Paul and his group want to preach in the province of Asia. For some reason, the Spirit prevents them from doing so. At that moment, there is no clear explanation of why. I have to believe that freely accepting any restriction was a serious challenge for Paul. After all, he was doing the Lord's work!

The text goes on to say that when they tried to enter Bithynia, "the Spirit of Jesus would not allow them to." These areas were a part of their ministry plans, serious plans to evangelize the region. We learn later that it was for the best of reasons that Paul was forced to wait. Because of his having to wait on his targeted area, he went down to Troas. As we might expect, Troas was exactly where the missionaries were supposed to be. While Paul was forced to wait there, he had a vision that would forever change the growth plan of the gospel in that part of the world.

In his vision, he was instructed to go to Macedonia and help start a series of new churches. This was not in Paul's original plan, and it took a brief period of waiting to bring it about. If Paul had not been restrained and had gone on with his original plan, this new work would never have been a reality, at least not due to Paul.

Is there anyone among us who has not had a good plan interrupted? Nothing is more difficult for us than to leave good work unfinished. This kind of experience is even more difficult when we believe our work is being done for the best of reasons. We might ask, "Why would God interrupt such generous and well-meaning plans?"

Service of Waiting

We must learn to accept that just as God calls us to the service of work, there are important times when He calls us to the service of waiting. God's call *to be* involves not only action but at times inaction. Those moments may even include isolation. How can such inactivity possibly be a good thing when we are so ready to get on with our plans? Yet, the harvest may be far richer in those silent, inactive moments than when we seem to be in full power and moving ahead.

Being Is Being Led

"Being" means allowing God to lead even when opportunities have been postponed and the doors seem closed. That is exactly what happened to Paul. If he had not been forced to wait, he would have never heard the call to Macedonia. The same is often true for each of us. Often the outcome is that in actively waiting we see another door that would never have been visible in the rush of activity. Resting secure on the confidence and trust of the One who works through us, we come to see that our best service may be that we are called to do nothing.

Do Not Despair

The psalmist knew well the challenge of waiting. In the twenty-seventh Psalm the writer's experience is described: "I would have despaired unless I had believed that I would see the goodness of the LORD. Wait for the LORD, be strong, and let your heart take courage" (Ps 27:13-14). The psalmist believed that at the end of waiting would be understanding of what God was trying to accomplish. God will be faithful.

We dare not forget one clear fact of life: Never overlook the reality that waiting provides an open window for despair. We become disheartened and our faith seems to stagger under the trials and testing that come into our lives. We may believe we cannot go any further or wait any longer. Even when we try not to despair, the temptation is great.

When we become tired and faint, we should do in our relationship with God what we have done at other times when we approached the end of our physical strength. What happens when we have been weak and physically incapable of doing anything? We come to terms with the fact that we have no choice but to depend upon someone else, to lean upon them. The answer is to lean upon the shoulder of a friend. While leaning upon them and depending upon them, we are granted the opportunity to cease and rest, trusting in another's strength.

Are we not to do the same in our relationship with God? When we reach the end of our own strength and ability, God does not say, "Be strong and courageous." The writer of Psalm 46 describes our instruction: "Be still and know that I am God." To follow that instruction is not passive surrender. It is not giving up or folding into the pressures of life. It is claiming the gift of waiting, which is being still and claiming the reassurance of God's presence.

Hudson Taylor was so weak and feeble in the last few months of his life that he told a friend, "I am so weak I cannot write. I cannot read my Bible. I cannot even pray. All I can do is lie still in the arms of God as a little child, trusting Him."[1]

Waiting is not passive surrender. Waiting is not life on hold. Waiting is a verb. It means using the moment to gain perspective, to lean on One who sees the unseen future, and to know that God has not forsaken. It means we claim our understanding of time is different than the clock God uses. Waiting is a verb. Waiting is not the enemy of life; it is the friend of being.

Note

[1] L.B.Cowman, *Streams in the Desert* (Grand Rapids MI: Zondervan, 1997), 188.

Chapter 6

Being:
Opening Our Senses

"Look at the birds of the air . . . ." —*Matthew 6:26a*

Solitude is not an enemy to be feared but an ally and friend in our response to God's call to be. In the previous pages, I described some of the lessons I learned in my slow dance with solitude in Westray, Scotland. Indeed, solitude was a friend that required some courtship, but at the same time it taught me so much. One additional discovery is well worth passing along, even worth the extra pages of this chapter.

This discovery became for me one of the most energizing dimensions of solitude, and it involves more than a little irony. Stated simply, in quiet and solitary moments I become less dependent on outside stimuli for the determining of my thoughts and actions and, at the same time, far more aware of the world around me. In becoming less dependent upon the outside world, I become more aware and deeply more appreciative of that same outside world.

First of all, there is nothing wrong with responding to the world around us. But the tendency in our over-stimulated lives is to ignore the world within, which is just as real as what we see, hear, and touch on the outside. The world within can be phenomenally exciting. But we tend to ignore it because usually we are too busy to notice. There is also too much noise to hear.

Think of a normal day. The easiest and quickest way to schedule our day is to depend totally on the outside demands that force their way into our lives. I speak from personal experience when I claim that it is much easier to hand over the routine of my day, to concede the determination of my actions, to the demands and expectations that come from other people and circumstances on the outside. Most of us do it without thinking about the process.

Take a day and make it your goal to notice how you spend your hours. How much of your day is determined by the people and circumstances that force their way into your life? Pay attention to why you do what you do. If you are honest, you will admit that most of your day is a response to the demands that come your way, demands that are both overt and subtle. Much of our behavior is a response to what is going on outside of us. Solitude can help us pay attention to why we do what we do. Our choices and decisions can be made from the inside out, rather than from the outside in. The more aware I become of the sense of being and life on the inside, the more my behavior can be initiated from within. At that point, an exciting discovery can be made, and this is where the irony comes to play.

One Becomes Alive

Solitude is more than just not having anyone around. Solitude is best when one is keenly aware that all the normal things that determine one's thoughts and actions are not in control. This awareness can, at times, be fatiguing. Mind and spirit must become engaged in a way that is not necessary when outside stimuli call the shots. What one thinks, does, and responds to becomes a conscious decision from within.

The surprising dimension of this discovery was that becoming more aware of the world within does not cut one off from the outside world. It is the opposite. The more we become aware of our need to be, the more we become in tune and even sensitive to the world outside. Instead of one's responses being forced by the outside, those responses become a choice, a deliberate decision. One does not disengage from the outside. The difference is that one is not controlled by it. The result is that eyes can be opened and ears become sensitive. There is no further need to defend one's self against the outside. One becomes free to respond to it or not. The result is that one's senses are opened.

The Perfect Model

From what we know of the life of Jesus, there is no better model to follow. Those on the outside never controlled His life. At the same time, He was never preoccupied with Himself or obsessed by His own needs. He simply never handed over the controls to other people. Yet, in living this way, He was always more sensitive and aware and ready to respond to the needs of people with whom He came into contact.

Notice how Jesus' senses were so tuned in to the needs of people around Him. He was keenly aware of what was going on all around Him. He was phenomenally responsive, yet He did so at his own choosing. The fifth chapter of Mark contains a classic example of Jesus' maintaining a level of awareness uncommon to most of us.

In the text, Jesus is in the midst of a terribly demanding day. He has just finished a journey with His disciples that required calming a storm. Upon reaching land, Jesus is approached by a man with an unclean spirit. The man cries for help from Jesus, and Jesus responds to his need. After crossing the lake once more, He is again met by a crowd. A man named Jairus steps forth and pleads with Jesus to come to his home and heal his sick daughter.

The text paints a vivid picture of a large crowd following Jesus, pressing Him from all sides. Yet, Jesus continues to direct His actions from within in spite of all the demands placed upon Him. The best evidence of it occurs as He continues to follow Jairus to his home. In the midst of all the demands, Jesus becomes aware of someone having touched Him. So aware of His own sense of being, He realizes that something is taken from Him. He turns around and asks, "Who touched my clothes?"

Even the disciples are astonished that with all the people pressing Him, He even notices or questions that someone has touched Him. But Jesus is so in touch with Himself that He knows something important has occurred. The woman falls at His feet and confesses that she touched Him. He tells her not to be afraid and to go in peace and be free from her suffering.

Then, Jesus continues with his journey toward the home of Jairus and meets the needs of the daughter by healing her. These events demonstrate an exceptional inner strength and awareness not common to most people. In spite of all the demands, Jesus continued to give Himself away. Operating from within did not make him insensitive to the needs of people around Him. In fact, the opposite occurred. He had more to offer.

Amazing Sensitivity

The part of that day in the life of Jesus that has intrigued me for a long time occurs in the middle of the story. I have long been fascinated with Jesus realizing that a woman had touched Him. In the midst of the pressures, Jesus knew something within Him had changed. The woman's touch would have gone unnoticed by anyone else. Certainly it would have been ignored by anyone operating solely from outside stimuli.

The ability Jesus possessed seemed to result from His being present in the current moment. He could have justifiably been caught up with all that had happened to Him that day, much of which He would not have intentionally included. He could have been playing back in His mind the points of the day that had been opposite of what He had planned. Frustration would have been a logical state of mind for Him.

He could just as easily have been anxious about the state in which He would find Jairus's daughter. Could all the delays have changed the potential for healing the daughter? We should not take the easy way out and assume that these distractions along the way would not influence the Son of God. The delays and unexpected circumstances along the way could not have gone unnoticed. Yet, Jesus' mind was obviously not filled with anxiety about how things would be when He arrived at the home of Jairus.

Instead, He was totally aware of Himself and totally given to the present moment. Being present to the moment seemed to characterize Jesus' way of doing life, and this experience was no different. So present was He that He knew someone had touched Him in a way that took something from Him. I think this story is an amazing example of being present to the present moment.

The Origin of His Awareness

I would never presume to have the one explanation as to why Jesus was able to be fully alive and present to the current moment. But I have to believe that high on the list of explanations would be the regular times He spent in communion with the Father and the moments of solitude when His senses were heightened and His strength renewed.

He constantly opened Himself to the Father to have His own resources replenished. He had much to give away, not just because He was divine, but because He disciplined Himself so that He had plenty to give away. He did it out of His motivation from within and not just in response to pressures from without.

I believe that the less we are aware of our own sense of being, the more likely we are to be overwhelmed by what is going on around us. We cannot give away something we do not have. And most of us try to give from a resource that is painfully empty. In the rush and "busyness," who has time for meditation and prayer? We pray like we treat fast food. We want it fast and with no waiting line. We want it on the go with one hand on the steering wheel. We have little to give because we spend little time in preparation.

The Origin of One's Actions

Much depends on the origin from which our behavior is prompted. If we are driven only by stimuli from without, the demands and pressures that come from every direction, then we claim little control or joy in our actions. On the other hand, if we maintain a sense of our own being and an awareness that we are not puppets with strings going to the outside, we can exercise control and respond in a way that is much more honorable to the One in whose image we are created.

A spark of divine within us longs to give to and improve our surroundings. If we are unaware of that piece of us, we totally hand over the controls of our lives to the events and circumstances that call upon us. Jesus was adept at exercising joy and pleasure in the most difficult of circumstances. Most of us find neither joy nor pleasure in most routine days.

Seeing with the Heart

The Apostle Paul describes in a beautiful way his hope for the people of the church in Ephesus. In 1:17 he prays that "the God of our Lord Jesus Christ may give you the Spirit of wisdom." I think it is interesting that in my translation the word *spirit* begins with a capital letter. But Paul goes on to use a phrase that I never appreciated until now. In verse 18, he writes, "I pray that the eyes of your heart may be enlightened in order that you may know the hope . . . ." I am intrigued by the imagery of the phrase "eyes of your heart." Until recent days, I have not appreciated that image.

As we search for the sense of being that lies underneath all the labels that define us, we can only accomplish that task with "eyes of the heart." Our eyes can only take us so far. There is a point where only the eyes of the heart can take over and help us understand who we are.

I am convinced that most of us have vision problems. The limitations we have with our sight are not found in our eyes. It is the "eyes of the heart" that need to be enhanced and developed. Joy in life depends on developing the ability to process life from the inside out instead of the reverse as our only option.

The Principle of Vacuum

A certain principle must acknowledged and respected in our struggle to be. Simply stated, it is the Principle of Vacuum. Even though it may not seem profound at first, this principle has everything to do with our responding to God's call to be.

St. Martin of Tours was one of the Celtic leaders of the church in the fourth century. He was phenomenally successful in converting huge numbers of pagans to Christianity. Part of the reason for his success was a particular strategy. In *Life of Martin*, Sulpitius Severus wrote an interesting description of him and his strategy:

> And truly before Martin's day, very few, hardly any of these regions had professed Christ, but now the Holy Name became so well known, thanks to the miracles and the example of Martin, that the whole district is full of churches and monasteries. Martin's practice being, wherever he destroyed heathen sanctuaries to replace them immediately with churches and monasteries.[1]

What catches my attention is the description of Martin's immediately replacing vacated heathen sanctuaries with a Christian presence—churches or monasteries. The people of his time had practiced pagan religions for ages. Their habits were well ingrained. Martin knew that as the movement of the gospel displaced pagan sites, something must be quickly created in their place or else people would revert back to their old ways. The law of the empire was that whenever a pagan temple fell into disuse, the property should be handed over to the empire for secular use.

Instead, Martin and his followers claimed this vacated space as outposts for the spread of the gospel. A Principle of Vacuum is acknowledged in this description of the way Martin went about his business. It is a safe assumption that even though the pagan practice disappeared from a site, if left long enough, some form of paganism would return. Why? It is the Principle of Vacuum.

This principle can be observed in many other ways. For example, a few weeks ago I spent an entire Saturday pulling weeds from shrubbery and flowerbeds. They were yanked, pulled, and extracted. It would have been nice if that were the end of the weeds. Did they disappear forever? You know the answer. I have not touched the beds since and, guess what, the weeds are coming back. Nature follows the principle of vacuum. We have a swimming pool in our yard. The water may be sparkling clear today, but the work is never finished. Let it go and what happens? One morning the water is green from algae. It was crystal clear a few days ago. Why did it turn green? The Principle of Vacuum.

The application of this principle to our journey of being is self-evident. Our minds are always working. They may not always work just as we please, but they are working nevertheless. If we are to truly respond to God's call to be, we must manage our minds better. We must give greater care as to what enters our minds.

In his book *Walking the Edges*, David Adam makes an interesting analogy: "In a sense the mind is like some great record. Everything you see, do, and experience is taped,ized, kept somewhere in your memory. It follows that the quality of the material you put on the tape is the quality of the material you will have for playback."[2]

If we want to protect the sacred spark within us, our genuine sense of being given by the Creator God, then we must be constantly vigilant of what we allow into our minds. The Apostle Paul had some appropriate comments about the same issue: "Finally, brothers, whatever is true, whatever is noble, whatever is right, whatever is pure, whatever is lovely, whatever is admirable—if anything is excellent or praiseworthy—think about such things" (Phil 4:8).

Notes

[1] Sulpitius Severus, *The Life of Martin*, vol. 11 (Alexander Roberts: James Parker, 1894), 146.

[2] David Adam, *Walking the Edges* (London: Holy Trinity Church: Society for Promoting Christian Knowledge, 2003), 59.

Chapter 7

Being: Paying Attention

He saw the crowds and had compassion. —Matthew 9:36

There is a practical result of opening our senses and being driven from within, as described in the previous chapter. The result is of an increased level of paying attention. The increased ability to pay attention may be one of our best spiritual upgrades. If you were given a score today on the test of "paying attention," what kind of marks would you receive?

Let me explain what I have in mind by sharing a personal frustration. It has to do with the way I go about my daily routine. My frustration comes from the fact that I constantly miss so much that ought to be obvious. What am I missing? These oversights are mostly simple, yet profoundly important. They are normal things, yet they add so much depth and joy to life. I miss them because I am mentally and emotionally somewhere else.

One of my best teachers on this issue is my granddaughter, whom I have already introduced to you. Let me give you an example of her instruction. One day recently she visited us. She wanted to go outside. If I picked her up and carried her, we could move faster and get it done faster. So, with her hooked to my side, we began our walk. We had been outside only for a minute or two when she excitedly pointed to a redbird. The bird was absolutely beautiful, filled with vibrant color. In all honesty, if my granddaughter had not pointed it out, I probably wouldn't have noticed.

Right after pointing to the bird, she pointed to a plane high in the sky that left a huge trail of white cloud behind it. Even late in the day, the sun shone through the stream of widening smoke and turned it into a beautiful, brilliant sight. The chances are good that I would not have noticed the plane either unless Ashlyn had pointed it out. I would like to think I was simply paying my usual, total attention to her. The chances were good, however, that I was thinking about all kinds of other things—making the mortgage payment, my schedule for the next day, or something else that probably had no long-term impact on my life. The fact remains that I was not paying much attention to my surroundings at that moment.

Another Lesson, A Noisy One

Another experience recently became a teachable moment for me. At the time of this writing, we have just concluded the Easter celebration. Our church, like many others, began the day with a sunrise service. If you are a preacher, a sunrise service creates a long day, but it does add a special dimension to the most important day of our church calendar. Sunday's early morning service offered several opportunities for paying attention. One was quite humorous and had nothing to do with the theme of the gathering. It was a vivid and noisy reminder that you can only exercise so much control over the environment in an outside setting. As the congregation sat and listened to the sermon, we all began to hear the distant noise of a flock of geese coming from the west.

There was no way to miss the moment. The honking of the geese could be heard for miles in advance. My guess is that we were all thinking the same thing at that moment—with all the territory to choose from, surely the geese would take a route that went away from our area. Wrong! Their honking grew closer and closer, and they literally flew directly overhead. My worse fear was that they might actually land and join us. Fortunately, they found a spot a few acres away on the other side of the church lot. Being still was not a requirement for paying attention to that part of the morning. However, it did add a special touch of ambiance to the early morning hour.

Sunrise

Another memory of that Easter morning was considerably more instructive for me. Even though I was, as one would expect, a participant in the service, there were some quality moments when I could sit still and give attention to the occasion and the environment. At the beginning of the service, there were some delightful and surprising moments of silence. During those brief moments I was able to do something I had not done in a long time. I sat in one spot and watched the dawning of the new day. It may seem like such a routine thing—the dawning of a day. After all, it occurs every morning. But, how often do I, we, pay close attention to the details of the transition?

I get up early almost every day, usually before the sun rises. In fact, customarily the time and the direction I turn out of my subdivision points me directly at the rising sun. Every day I am re-impressed with its beauty. On the other hand, it is also the same time I am usually managing a cup of coffee and trying to keep all my things orderly in the seat as I begin my commute to the office. It goes without saying that I am not giving much attention to the rising sun, other than passing notice that another day has begun.

But Easter Sunday morning was different. I sat in one spot, listening, observing and taking it all in. There were no big surprises, and it is not like I have not watched it happen before. I guess I just forget from one time to another how magnificent the transition is. The transition from darkness to daylight is an amazing change. The birds come alive as they sing aloud. Something so simple as the utility light that normally illumines the area gently gives way to the increase of the sun's warmth, power, and brilliance. The world awakens to a new day, and the transition is magnificent. I had forgotten how much happens as the night submits to the power of the day.

Could it be that special effects were added because it was Easter? As special as Easter morning may be, the truth is that this same show takes place every morning. I just don't pay attention to it. Or at least I don't give myself the opportunity. I am always busy doing something else and miss it.

Observing the sunrise that morning created no major changes in my life. There was no dramatic difference as a result of that experience. On the other hand, my life experience of that day was enriched. We pass up so many experiences that add depth to our lives because we simply do not notice them. The sunrise service forced me to do something I do not do well—sit still and pay attention. Who has time to pay attention?

Jesus Tried to Help

The New Testament records several times when Jesus in His teachings tried to help us pay better attention. He was a good example. He seemed so alert and aware. He noticed things and people that others failed to see. Many of His illustrations indicate how in touch with surroundings He was. Do you remember what He said to His disciples in Luke 12? Evidently the disciples were anxious, probably scurrying around as we do much of the time. For one thing, Jesus came right out and said, "Stop worrying." He encouraged them to look around and learn from nature. Check out the lilies and the birds, He told them. They don't seem to be uptight.

Jesus went on to point out how the lilies grow. He said, "They do not toil or spin." The phrase "toil and spin" has always intrigued me. It may best describe how most of us live. In fact, it sounds awfully close to the scurrying most of us know too well. I do not think Jesus is suggesting an attitude of laziness. The flowers and birds are not lazy; they are simply doing what they were put here to do.

The lilies of which Jesus spoke were abundant on the hills. All of his listeners would have quickly perceived their familiar beauty. When rain came, the flowers would quickly open and receive the water and be a source of beauty. They were never too busy to take in the rain. They simply took in what was provided for them. Remaining closed and waiting until the next rain was not an option.

Personally, I gain more from the image of the birds than I do the flowers. I am no expert on the habits of birds. However, what I find most amazing is how responsive they are to the conditions around them. On that Easter morning, long before the sun came within view, the birds were already singing. Have you ever noticed that when you toss breadcrumbs out, the birds quickly respond to your offering? I enjoy feeding the birds in our backyard. Often I toss birdseed to them early in the morning. What I find entertaining is that they respond to the presence of the seed before I can even get back to the house. They seem to be so in tune with their surroundings. They never seem too busy to respond to the moment. In spite of the risks of comparing ourselves to birds, the truth is that most of the time we are not responsive or in touch with our surroundings at all.

So Very, Very Practical

What Jesus is teaching us is both theological and intensely practical. When was the last time you smelled the rain? When was the last sunset you actually stopped to watch? When driving your car, when did you last notice all the scenes you passed? In all honesty, I notice little because in my mind I am already where I plan to go. Most of my attention is on the drivers who are slowing me down.

One day recently I was listening to my radio while traveling in my car. The program was a news-talk format and the person was talking about the beauty of spring. He asked, "With spring all around, are you looking at it in color?" My first reaction was that it was a silly question. But as I looked around, I promise you it was the first time I really saw the rich green of new leaves and the brilliant color of budding trees. Up to that moment, I had paid no attention. Where in the world had I been?! The answer is lots of places, but obviously one of them was not the present moment.

I believe Jesus is trying to help us be more fully alive to the world around us. Jesus teaches several practical lessons in this story from Luke.

(1) Don't forget that Jesus' advice follows a teaching about being overly concerned with material things. He did not say material things are demonized, only that we should be careful. Otherwise, material things will own us and totally occupy our minds. Material concerns can easily consume us. A few verses back in the same passage, Jesus responds to a man who asks Him to help settle an inheritance dispute in his family. Among other things, Jesus quickly identifies the presence of greed. Greed can fill our thought process with so much concern over material things. Not all concern is the result of greed, but the fact remains that "things" can dominate our conscious process if we are not careful.

(2) Seek the Kingdom first. Seek Kingdom things first. That has to do with our priorities. Let the Kingdom guide us. Give our best to life. We are not to be slackers and bums. We are to do our best in everything.

(3) Having done our best, leave the rest to God. Trust Him. Make it more than just songs we sing or platitudes we express. Make it the base of our lives. I am convinced that doing our best and leaving the rest to God has more to do with positive mental health than anything else we can ever do. Most of us, however, never learn that truth. We do our work and then we "toil and spin." We never simply turn it over to the One we claim to trust.

Implication

The implications of our inattentiveness are obvious, with both theological and practical applications. For example, on a personal level, think of all the experiences we miss due to our inattentiveness. Most of these experiences are not the difference between life and death. They simply add joy and enrichment to life. The cute dance your child does when hearing a song on the radio may not change anything in your life. The funny hat your spouse wears when you arrive earlier than expected will not provide a picture for the family Bible, but it may be one of the memories that lingers in the mind when even more profound experiences have faded from memory. Our missing such experiences has nothing to do with our checking account or our 401K retirement fund. It has everything to do with losing out on something that adds depth and joy to life. We miss so much because we are not paying attention.

Other Examples

Jesus consistently demonstrated this inner sense of being and awareness by noticing things others would ignore. By operating from within, He noticed flowers and birds and made beautiful object lessons of them. The flow of His actions was from within to without, and He operated with sensitivity and awareness that is only a dream to most of us.

In another experience in the twelfth chapter of Mark, Jesus is leading His disciples through Jerusalem. They slowly pass the temple, and just being there overwhelms the disciples. Their stimulation from without is so great that all they see are the big and obvious things around them. As they watch the wealthy people of that day place bags of money on the altar, the disciples are apparently taken by the sight. Yet what does Jesus see and call attention to? He notices a widow offering her two simple copper coins. In fact, Jesus is so impressed that He demands that the disciples pay attention to the level of her sacrifice. They adjust their focus from the overwhelming big picture to pay attention to the small but instructive picture of the poor widow.

Once again, it goes back to Jesus' incredible ability to operate from within and not be overwhelmed by the demands and circumstances that called upon Him. His ability to be present to the current moment is not the norm for most of us. I should only speak for myself, but I am easily given to the demands that come my way. All too often my actions are totally determined by the latest demand that falls in front of me.

Opportunities for Service

When we habitually do not pay attention, we also miss out on many opportunities to contribute to life around us. How can we be of help when we are not paying attention? I think of the experience of Jesus when He was summoned to the home of Jarius. The passage describes Jesus as moving through the pressing crowds. In the midst of the crowd pressing Jesus from every side, He is aware that someone has touched Him. How could He have even noticed? But He did, and He stopped to inquire and offer help. Even His disciples questioned Jesus about why He should inquire. The poor and needy were all around Him. I find that story of our Lord absolutely amazing, especially the way He paid attention to a simple, unnamed woman in need.

For those of us who follow Christ and claim to share His mission in the world, how can we be effective if we do not see? Dr. Peter Storey was pastor of the one of the premier churches in Johannesburg, South Africa, during the days of the Apartheid. His church was an all-white congregation. Dr. Storey's mission as pastor was to make his church reflective of the population. Far from just changing the racial structure of the church, he longed for his congregation to be more informed and sympathetic to the racial inequalities of his nation. In a lecture to a group at Duke Divinity School, he described the prerequisite for any significant change in his church as the necessity of opening his congregation's eyes.[1]

An Absolute Fact

It is an absolute fact that we can only be of service to the extent that we see. A descriptive picture is painted of Jesus in Matthew 9:36 in the simple words, "He saw the crowds and had compassion." I have come to the point of believing that the most important word in that passage is *saw*. Jesus' seeing preceded His caring. How can we care and demonstrate our sharing of the Lord's mission if we do not see?

If we are to be attentive to the needs of people around us, we must pay attention. If we are to share genuinely in the mission of Jesus, we must be able and willing to see. Paying attention is an absolute requirement for being of service to our Lord and the people for whom He died. There is so much that we do not see. We are somewhere else. And just as those personal enriching experiences are gone forever, so are the opportunities for compassion and service.

Many Moments Come Only Once

When we ignore the discipline of practicing the presence of God and also ignore the practicing of our own presence, we miss moments that come only once. How many times have we ignored the beauty of a rainbow, wanting to quickly finish the task that engages us for the moment? We put away the voice within that says we should stop and drink deeply from the present moment. We continue to be driven from without and, more times than not, we miss the rainbow. It is not there when we finally get around to paying attention. The moment is missed forever. The rainbow that could have fed our inner spirit was forever postponed.

We awaken in the morning, and all that is in our heads is the schedule that we anticipate for the day. Something within tells us to postpone our departure for the rat race for a few moments and become aware of ourselves and God's Spirit, which longs to work through us during the day. In spite of our sensing a need to do otherwise, we jump into our day, aware only of all the demands lined up to take their shot at us.

There is also the possibility that a need will make its way to us on that same day, a need that God has specifically given us the ability to meet. But, because we are operating only from without, we are unaware that we have exactly the resource to address the need. God planned to use us that day, but no inner sense of being gave us the clue that we were a part of the plan.

Personal God Moments

When we are inattentive, we not only miss experiences that enrich our lives and opportunities for living out the mission we claim to embrace, but we also miss moments for God to move close and give meaning to our lives. Our souls ache for sacred moments when we sense God's presence. Yet, those moments cannot always be scheduled to meet our personal routine. Sometimes they occur at the most unexpected times.

There are times when we experience sacred thin places that have been scheduled on our calendar. At times, these moments can be arranged to meet our personal schedules. A thin place is any mystical place where the distance between heaven and earth is small. Recently I accompanied our church college group on a mission trip to Denver, Colorado. There was one predictable thin place. On the last night of the mission week, we gathered for Communion on the side of a mountain overlooking Denver, the city where we had served. As we remembered the experiences of the past week, we looked from our mountain view at the areas of the city where we had ministered. Taking the bread and the cup was phenomenally meaningful in that setting. Yet, knowing the view would be spectacular, I anticipated that this would be a thin place.

There were so many other God moments during the week that I would not have been able to predict. Working in a soup kitchen in downtown Denver, I handed a plate of food to a man who was dirty and terribly unkept. He looked me in the eye and said, "Thanks for caring." All I had done was show up at the soup kitchen. But somehow God spoke to me through the simple words of that unkempt man. During a week when I seriously questioned if all our work was amounting to anything, the words of that man were from another source. The source reminded me that simple acts do count. Such a simple experience, but a God moment that I would have missed if I had only been concerned to pour the next glass of tea for the next unnamed homeless person in line.

I long for encounters with God. My soul absolutely aches for those moments that add meaning and joy to my life. Some of them I can encourage and help bring about by being in certain places at certain times. Formal worship takes place every Sunday morning. Ignoring that opportunity for encounter is like pushing away food when you're hungry. But God is not limited to scheduled appearances. He often moves toward us in the simplest ways. Sometimes it happens in the voice of a colleague who speaks to us at just the right time. Sometimes it happens in the silence of the early morning when no one else is up and busy. It can happen at any time, and my understanding is that God seems to prefer to move close to us in unexpected moments. The truth is that they often happen to us when we least expect them and are most unprepared. Therefore, paying attention is so important if there is a genuine hunger for unpredictable God moments.

The Enemy of Being

I am relatively certain that our "call to be" has no greater enemy than our inattentiveness to the present moment. When Jesus talks about toiling and spinning, I think he refers to anxious thought and endless activity. In no way was Jesus ordering a man or woman to be reckless and lazy. We are expected to do our best, give our best effort, and then leave the rest to God.

Jesus makes it clear that a person is expected to give priority to the Kingdom of God. Seek that Kingdom first. Seeking the Kingdom is present tense. Just do the right thing and do your best, then trust God for that which you can never fully control. The "call to be" is difficult, if not impossible, when frantic activity and anxiety constantly characterize your life.

Our attention is seldom to the current moment. And we miss so much. Often it is the little things, like the smile of a child, the dawn that changes to the morning sun, the evening that passes through the sunset and displays colors only God can create. In a matter of moments, those experiences are gone, and when they are gone, they are gone forever. One either takes them in at the moment or not at all.

"Being" requires attention, especially attentiveness. Toiling and spinning are constant enemies of being.

Note

[1] Peter Storey, *With God in the Crucible* (Nashville: Abingdon Press, 2002), 45.

Chapter 8

Being:
God Tried to Help Us

"Remember the Sabbath day . . . ." —*Exodus 20:8a*

In a recent conversation with a colleague, I discussed my plans for this book. I offered my capsule explanation of why I think being must precede doing. My colleague responded with a jesting tone, "Who has time to *be*? You've got to be kidding!" I realize he was mostly joking, but he was speaking the truth. Being will always pose a challenge for us because there is so much to do. Being is not an enemy to doing. In fact, it is the best thing going for effective doing. A sense of being provides energy, focus, and meaning. Yet my friend is right: "Who has time anymore just to *be*?"

Is the challenge unique to our era? No. Is it worse than in previous times? Absolutely!

Even a superficial look at the biblical account indicates that God knew we would face a challenge at this point. From the beginning,

God knew the challenge would be more than we could manage on our own. One important rule was given to us with our best interests in mind. Of course, we pay little attention to that rule today. It is the fourth commandment, "Remember the Sabbath day by keeping it holy."

This commandment seems at first like a benign suggestion, at least from the viewpoint of today's culture. It sounds out-of-date to most people. Our generation, if they are familiar with the commandment at all, evidently does not attach much validity to it. On the other hand, we should not overlook the way generations of Bible times took it seriously. Numbers 15:32 certainly makes it more than a suggestion, declaring that if a man is found gathering wood on the Sabbath contrary to the Lord's command, he should be stoned to death by the community. Today's ACLU would have a court circus with that law!

Even though Jesus made it clear that the people of His day had misunderstood the intent of the fourth commandment, His intent was simply to change the understanding of the Sabbath from a law to a gift. In his book *Reinventing Sunday*, Brad Berglund has made an interesting observation: "The message of that ancient society is clear—stop working or die. It is the opposite of modern society's message, which is 'stop working and die.'"[1]

Society's Demands

There is little value in engaging in a debate as to whether Sunday has been crowded to the point of being just another day. The truth is obvious; it's a given fact. Sunday now offers little difference from any other day of the week. Granted, it is a part of the weekend and the weekend has developed a life of its own. However, it seems to me that the weekend philosophy of today relates little to the original design of the Sabbath.

As a baby boomer, I have witnessed most of this change occur in my lifetime. The Sunday routine of today's culture looks nothing like that of my childhood, and it is far more than the demise of the church culture we once knew. Do not hear me saying that in the world of my childhood everyone went to church. Not even close! In my memory, a higher percentage did attend church than today, but the difference in that day and today is far more systemic.

Even for those who did not attend church, there was a basic respect for the Sabbath, our Sunday. They may have slept in on Sunday morning or spent the day on the golf course, but there was no concerted, wholesale competition created for attention and focus on the Sabbath. In times past, there was more opportunity "to be," even if you had no interest in church.

Today is dramatically different, and not just because of the usual National Football League game on Sunday or the Masters Golf Tournament that occurs on Easter. In the grand scheme of things, those events affect the lives of only a minority of families. Instead, I am talking about the routine, regularly scheduled events that swallow a family's energy and attention on Sunday. Not too long ago, I heard of a few soccer leagues beginning to schedule an occasional game on Sunday afternoon. Then it was the exception and not the norm. But the exception soon became the norm, and Sunday morning turned into the prime time of the week for local sporting events. Many parents found themselves in the position of having to choose between supporting their children's sporting life and showing up for church. Many tried to do both, even if it meant being totally fatigued on Sunday night, with standard Monday morning pressures staring them in the face. Monday would inherently begin with a sense of fatigue and lack of focus, like playing a basketball game with no timeouts.

Circumstances of Sunday sports are even more the norm for today's families. Parents don't want to embarrass their children or themselves by potentially being isolated for the sake of a rule written long ago and for anther culture. Even if they don't articulate it, many parents are aware that in some way values are just as much an issue as excelling in a particular sport. Yet nobody wants to be perceived by friends as a religious fanatic, so they just do their best and explain it away in the name of parental support. Then the routine moves further away from Sunday respect. It is not enough to schedule local games; now parents encourage their children to participate in up-grade leagues, whose games are mostly played out of town. The family not only drives across town on Sunday. They drive across the state, often leaving on Saturday. So much for family-friendly activity and dialogue on the weekend. Instead, the mantra becomes, "Get your bags. Get in the car. Everybody just be still and quiet. We will rest while we drive."

A Complicated Issue

Many issues emerge around our culture's use of Sunday, too many to deal with in this short space. For example, how much of the hectic activity of the weekend is the desire of our children, and how much of it is our less-than-subtle pressure on them to excel? A healthy competitive spirit within our children can be good thing. Often, though, we press them beyond their own desires so that we might vicariously experience success through them.

The sports life of our children and youth is only a small part of our continued ignoring of the Sabbath. The fourth commandment refers to working on the Sabbath. In our culture, that issue opens a huge can of worms. If six days of productivity is good, seven days is much better. In a culture where success is the supreme god, seven days of productivity are hard to reject. When our value is determined by our productivity and success becomes the ultimate affirmation, who can refuse the lure of the seventh day?

This whole culture of the way we abuse, ignore, and deny the Sabbath gift is a web of complication. Do a philosophical MRI or CAT scan of our society's use of Sunday, and you will find many indications of the cancer eating away at our personal and family health. Who has time to think introspectively or retrospectively, journey inward, or just be still when there is so much to do and so many reasons to do it?

Not a Law, but a Gift

In our rushed lifestyle, we are ignoring one of God's most special gifts. The Sabbath was never meant to be a set of chains, never meant to be restrictive. Instead, it was designed to enhance life, give meaning to existence, and, most of all, encourage us to be. From the beginning, the observance of the Sabbath was to provide rest and revitalization after a demanding week of doing.

The Genesis account, chapter 2, describes with clarity the purpose of the seventh day. After the heavens and earth were finished, God rested on the seventh day. If work is to have a diminishing effect on body and spirit, provision must be made for the replenishing of those physical and spiritual energies. The gift of the Sabbath was God's attempt at providing for one of the most basic of human needs—rest. This rest is for more than simply replenishing our muscles. Rest is a mental process that allows us to move close to the center of life, that sacred space that is never known by the usual rushed and hectic lifestyle.

As a result of the resurrection of Christ, the Christian community embraced Sunday, the first day of the week, as the Sabbath day of rest. Our Sabbath was no longer just a day of physical restraint. The celebration and worship that followed the Lord's resurrection incorporated a much-needed spiritual dimension to rest. Sabbath, at its best, was designed to replenish both our physical and spiritual energies. To ignore such an opportunity borders on foolishness.

Misunderstood and Abused

Because our society has ignored the inherent benefits of God's provision, we are weaker. As stated previously, the secular world ignores the provision of Sunday, and generally speaking the religious community borders on indifference. The establishment of a day of rest is not the result of human decision-making but the result of a divine ordinance.

The original observance goes beyond superficial practice. The twenty-third chapter of Exodus states emphatically that one's ox and colt must be given the opportunity for rest. The fifth chapter of Deuteronomy includes one's servants as having the right to Sabbath rest. As is the possibility with any observance, orthodoxy became the primary issue. The restrictions became so rigid that they cramped life within the system. The practice of the Sabbath became so excessive that rest gave way to confinement. The observance was obviously carried too far when rabbis began to debate whether a cripple were guilty if his house caught on fire on the Sabbath and he had to carry out his wooden leg.

Pharisees of the first century were wrong, and Jesus exposed them for what they were, lifeless as sepulchers. Francis of Assisi was right when he said, "Sadness belongs to the devil and his angels, but we, knowing what we know, and believing what we believe, what can we do except rejoice!" The Christian community has at times reflected some of the same legalism of the Jewish Sabbath. The Puritans of New England could easily have been first cousins to the first century Jewish scribes and Pharisees. Much of what we are experiencing today is a reaction to the excess of our Puritan predecessors.

In an effort to get away from rabbinical and puritanical inflexibility, most people have disregarded the value of a day of rest as God's gift to a tired humanity. Yet, the original value of the Sabbath is still the same. One cannot work indefinitely. One not only needs rest from labor but also a fresh perspective. The Sabbath is the best chance in the week for looking beyond the obvious, material dimension of life.

In Jesus' Eyes—A Gift

Jesus took a practical and wise approach to the Sabbath. He assisted people in need, as well as using the day as a time to refresh His own inner spirit, His sense of being. One resource for His strength was found in His customary presence in the synagogue on the Sabbath. In other words, Jesus went to church! Don't overlook that fact.

In the second chapter of Mark, Jesus tries to readjust our thinking about the Sabbath. People were not created to be slaves of the Sabbath. Instead, the Sabbath was created for the benefit of people. Adults and children alike need to free themselves from the need to do. It is a day that should not be measured by normal standards of productivity. It is a day when, as demonstrated by our Lord, we seek to restore both the physical and spiritual energies that have been depleted by the demands of the week.

As with all gifts, the value of the Sabbath is determined by the wisdom with which we receive it. A gift may be offered with the wisest of intentions. Yet, unless a gift is claimed, it has little value. God blessed the seventh day and made it sacred in itself, and He offers it to us as a source of well-being. When we ignore it or abuse it, we are diminished in the process.

Reasons for Disregard

The issues that emerge around the disregard and abuse of the Sabbath are complex and symptomatic of many of the ills of our society. Therefore, the reasons for our culture's neglect of the Sabbath are too many to consider in this short space. However, some obvious reasons can easily be acknowledged.

One reason is that we possess a natural tendency to overreact. We may reject the puritanical straightjacket and, in so doing, we go to the other extreme and lose sight of the gift altogether. To ignore the Sabbath is just as foolish as turning it into a prison sentence.

A second reason for our disregard is that many of us have consciously or unknowingly relinquished the control of Sunday. We have taken a passive approach to the issue. If we can assume the role of victim, we can avoid dealing with it altogether, or so it seems. Making use of the Sabbath in the way it was intended requires us to be better time managers. Claiming the role of victim saves me a lot of energy in re-prioritizing my life!

A third reason focuses on our pushing for productivity beyond the level of common sense. No one is suggesting that we become lazy and nonproductive. Yet, we ignore the practical dimension of this obsession. The foolishness can be found in the disregard for routine maintenance. The finest of equipment must be periodically idle for repair. Our bodies and our spirits are no different. Put the most expensive car on the road and ignore its maintenance. What happens? The result is that sooner or later even the most expensive car will leave you stranded.

A fourth reason may be the most difficult to label and, quite possibly, the most challenging to address. It has to do with our discomfort in being still. Taking regular time to focus on our sense of being requires that we periodically, if not weekly, be still. This sounds simple enough, but it forces us into the company of the one person we most often try to avoid—ourselves. If we can keep ourselves busy, overcommitted, and constantly in motion, we might be able to keep away from ourselves.

So, What Can We Do?

In response to this Sabbath dilemma, or rather the absence of Sabbath, what choices do we have? We *do* have choices. Many of those choices require changes in our lifestyles; in some cases, they will force us to go against the cultural flow of habit and thought.

One choice is to do nothing. Just fold our arms and claim no power to change anything about our lives and habits. Assuming the victim's position requires little from us. It does not put us on the spot. It does not force us to assume a position contrary to our friends and colleagues. Continuous damage control is always an option for us, even if it leaves us with the legitimate question, "Is this all life has to offer?"

A second choice is to look honestly at the way we currently perceive and use Sundays. Are we willing to claim Sunday as a gift? Are we willing to use it differently and be a better steward of it? In what ways am I connecting myself to spiritual resources on that day as well as giving my body physical rest? This does not mean spending the whole day at church. Given the chance, we who are in the church business can keep you busy enough on Sunday to tire you just as much as the sporting routine. It all boils down to claiming ownership of Sunday and being intentional about its use.

A third option may the selection of another time for your Sabbath. Some professions and occupations allow no choice but to work on Sunday. If a member of my family gets sick, I am grateful for those who work in the emergency room. When forced to travel on Sunday, my car welcomes gasoline and those who make it available. If you do not have much of an option on Sunday, claim another day. Seize another time and use it for needed revitalizing exercises. Claim some time and focus on your sense of being instead of on what you are doing.

The main response is to be intentional and not passive. You may not be able to change the larger world around you, but you can change the immediate world that touches you. You can point fingers at political parties or the media and blame them for the loss of values that once characterized us as a culture. Or you can claim ownership of your life and the lives of those for whom you are responsible and create new habits. We are creatures of habits, but habits can be changed. First, however, there must be a need to change.

Symptomatic of So Much More

The lack of a Sabbath is just one dynamic in a cultural dilemma that will ultimately have far-reaching consequences. Our Sunday-less culture is a symptom of a society that is too busy and overly-committed. The development of a sense of being that adds meaning to doing is a luxury few people can afford today. It takes time, and who has time? There is too much to be done. The result is that people are becoming strangers to each other, to God, and to themselves. God tried to help us. Long ago He told us to stop regularly and pay attention to why we have been working all the other days of the week. Meaning is found in our sense of being, and being precedes doing. Maybe the best way to deal with the lack of meaning is to step up the pace. After all, we will have more to show for our efforts. Or will we?

Note

[1] Brad Berglund, *Reinventing Sunday* (Valley Forge: Judson Press, 2001), 15.

Chapter 9

Being: Claiming Your Name

He calls his own sheep by name. —John 10:3

Do we appreciate the value, even the power, of a name? It is more than just a label attached to us after our birth. In many ways our names become synonymous with our personhood. It is among the first gifts offered at our birth, and it remains unchanged after our death.

Do you remember the encounter of Moses with God on Mount Sinai in Exodus 3:15? When Moses considered going to the people on behalf of God, the one thing he wanted most of all was to be able to give the name of one sending him. Being able to refer to this God by name would give Moses and God validity. Without a name, the task would be much harder.

Even God was synonymous with His name. In 1 Kings 5, "The temple will be built in my name." In 2 Chronicles, God's people are "called by my name." Even Jesus said, "where two or three come together in my name, there am I with them" (Matt 18:20).

There is power to be experienced in knowing someone's name. An interesting exchange is described in Mark 5. Jesus heals a demon-possessed man. Did you notice that when Jesus commanded the demon to come out of the man, Jesus asked the demon for its name? Why did Jesus need to know the name of the demon? In Jesus' day there was an assumption that to know someone's name was to have a certain amount of power in relation to that person. Knowing the demon's name gave Jesus even more power over it. This assumption in Bible times may also explain why God was reluctant to give Moses His name in the encounter on Mount Sinai.

Knowing and calling someone by his or her name is more than a courtesy. It is the way we move the closest to the core of an individual. Our names become a part of our identities. What begins as a label attached early in our lives quickly becomes far more.

So What?

What's in a name? Is it more than just a way of separating us so the post office can deliver our tax notices? Even more importantly, can a name give us something to claim that is underneath the normal labels on which we usually depend for our identity? After all, a name is given to us. Generally speaking, we do nothing to earn it. It usually becomes a part of who we are at the time of our birth.

Nicknames are different from our given names. We acquire nicknames because of something we do. Most nicknames are earned. They come from a particular trait of our personality or something we do by which we tend to be remembered. I remember an acquaintance from years ago who was called Smut. His name came from an experience long ago when we was too young to walk and somehow got smut on his face from the fireplace. Hence, he became known as Smut. It was something he did. Some nicknames are picked up earlier than others.

A high school classmate of mine was called Ox. It was never meant in disrespect. In fact, the truth is that he was strong as an ox. He played all sports and was the same in each one—strong. His nickname, Ox, was complimentary and definitely pointed to a trait he earned. That is the way of nicknames.

Our given name says more about our parents and/or our ancestors than it does about us. For our first name, our parents, for whatever reason, chose a name that suited them. In most cases it has little or nothing to do with anything we have done or any particular trait. It is definitely more of something we inherit than something we earn. At the same time, inheriting a name does not make it unimportant. Our last name often ties us to sources that give our lives meaning and understanding.

Biblical Names

In terms of the history of the human race, people have not had first and second names for long. Even if individuals were known by only one name, that one name often connected them to those they claimed as family. For example, names in the Bible can be informative, connecting a person to the past and symbolizing inheritance from a previous generation. For example, a few names begin with the phrase "Bar." When "Bar" appears in the front of a male name, it usually connects that individual to one's father. For example, Simon Barjonah means Simon, son of Jonah. He did nothing to earn that name. It was a gift from his birth, but the name is important because it describes an inheritance that comes with birth.

One well-known exception to that practice was the one whose name appears so many times in the book of Acts. His name was Barnabas, which literally means "son of encouragement." Unquestionably, Barnabas earned his name. Repeatedly, he appears at critical times, offering encouragement and injecting hope at the right moment. Barnabas had a way of showing up at critical moments when hope and encouragement were desperately needed.

A Name Well Deserved

When the church struggled for survival, Barnabas sold property and, as the Scripture describes, laid the money at the feet of the apostles.

This act infused hope into the lives of struggling members of this new group called The Way. Then, when Paul changed sides, literally doing a 180-degree turn, who showed up? Barnabas took him by the hand and stood up for him in the presence of the apostles. Later, as Paul and Barnabas planned their next missionary journey, the suggestion was made that they take John Mark with them. Paul said, "No." On an earlier journey, John Mark had returned home, which was evidently a huge source of frustration to Paul. When the request came for John Mark to rejoin them, Paul would not agree. Who offered encouragement? Barnabas. He said he would take John Mark with him, and Paul could take Silas as his partner.

So, Barnabas has a nickname, but it comes from the age-old practice of the prefix "bar." In his case, it meant "son of encouragement." I can think of few people whose name more reflects a positive attribute of personality than this man who disappeared into the times of the early church.

Surnames Adopted

Around the time of the fourteenth century, people received only one name. The obvious reason for adding a second name was the need for separating people with the same name. In every country and culture, certain names were frequently repeated. For example, it has been estimated that in medieval England three of every five men were named Henry, Robert, John, William, or Richard. Separating this many men with the same name became a challenge. Thus, the need for a second name became necessary. Second names were usually claimed in one of four ways.

Patriarchal

Surnames were adopted that connected one with his or her father. In a way that was similar to biblical times of adding "bar" in front of a name, "son" was attached to the end of the father's name and added to one first name. One's first name may have been Robert, but the second name became Peterson in connection with the father, Peter. The next generation kept the same family name.

Later, another naming process developed. According to Kristine Elliott, "The 'son' could also be understood by the position in the name. So, Richard's son Martin might be called Martin Richards instead of Martin Richardson. At the same time, Henry's son Martin might be know as Martin Henry, because to the medieval mind the position of the name Henry would imply that Martin was Henry's son. Other cultures used different ways of indicating patronymics. In Scotland and Ireland, the typical patronymic form was MacX, yielding names such as MacAndrew, MacDougall, MacGregor, and MacLeod."[1]

Occupation

Surnames were frequently derived from one's occupation or the occupation of one's father. It does not take a rocket scientist to figure out why so many people have the last name *Smith*. Climb up their genealogical tree far enough and you will discover a past family member, long ago, who was a goldsmith, leathersmith, silversmith, or some other type of smith.

While this name may have resulted from something one did in the first generation, it would soon become part of the inheritance of those who followed. Names provide enormous meaning to life when you think of them as inheritance. Someone named Smith today may have no connection to a particular trade except that they are connected to the rich history of one who did. One whose name currently is Smith may have no obvious skills as such, but a rich inheritance of the past gives meaning and value to the present.

Thus appear the last names of Baker, Tailor, Butler, and so many others. We often fail to appreciate the past history being revealed. Claiming a connection to the past becomes a valued part of the inheritance one can claim. It becomes a connection to the past and offers a gift to one's being. One does nothing to earn it. One can only claim it and add value to simply being who one is.

Nicknames

Even though we have already mentioned the illustrative value of nicknames, do not overlook the fact that many last names were the result of a nickname. At some point an individual became associated with a second name based on personality or a particular characteristic. This explains the familiar names of Long, Short, White, and Brown. Other names derived from the nickname. Easley may have come from a person many generations ago who was known as Easy.

According to Kristine Elliott, "An appellation of this sort can be complimentary, uncomplimentary, or simply descriptive. Nicknames can take various forms: descriptive of physical characteristics of some kind like Armstrong or descriptive of character or mental or moral characteristics, such as Wastepenny, Slyman, Careless, Bonfaith. Sometimes a nickname can be metaphoric (i.e., "John is like a . . ."), yielding names like Peppercorn for a small person and Fairweather for a cheerful, sunny person."[2]

Even though it may have referred to a specific individual at the beginning, the second name was also passed on to the children. While the nickname did not apply to them personally, it certainly connected them to an individual of that characteristic in the past.

Toponymics

Another practice in the naming process is the way names were often indicative of location, at least of one's ancestors. It is hard for us to understand the identification of names with location because we are so mobile today. But, in times past, people did not stray far from their places of origin. Families generally stayed in the same place. They occupied the same dwelling places. Generations would live under the same roof. Particularly, families and clans were connected to the place of their origin. They would often take that location as a part of their name.

Kristine Elliott offers insight into the naming process. She points out that "locatives are typical of the aristocracy in England and France. . . .Typical forms in Old English and Middle English are aet x, atte x, de x, of x. For example aet Lintone, atte Homwode, de London, de

Ebor. Sometimes the name of the place followed the given name directly, without a preposition."3

The name might actually appear as "Someone" from "a Place." The name may have started as John from Williamshire, meaning John was from the family or clan that had Williamshire as its origin. For the sake of brevity, the name may eventually be shortened to John Williams. Regardless, the connection with a location of a past ancestor explains surnames like Woods, Hill, or Lake. They simply identify a person's place of origin.

On a Personal Note

One reason I know of this possibility is that my own name had its origin in a similar kind of circumstance. I want to share a recent experience that not only helps me understand the origin of my family, but also gives meaning to my life, or in the terms of this book, my sense of being. I hope my story will offer encouragement to you to claim your name as a significant part of your being.

All my life I have heard the stories from my parents' generation of the origin of the Cadenhead name. According to rather accurate research done by a number of individuals, the first Cadenhead came from Scotland in the mid-eighteenth century. The stories agree that Cadenhead was a merchant sailor and docked in either the Charleston or Savannah harbor. While his boat was there, it caught fire and burned. John was killed in the fire. His son James was with him and chose to remain in America.

James fought in the Revolutionary War and then was recorded as owning two hundred acres in Pitt County, North Carolina. His grave to this day is inscribed "James Cadenhead, A Revolutionary Soldier." Since that time our family has located the graves of all our grandfathers, including William Pew Cadenhead, who fought for the Confederate Army in the Civil War. From our grandfathers' side of the family we can trace our roots from this moment all the way to John who first came from Scotland.

Having successfully connected our family line to this sailor from Scotland, could it be taken back further? One of my uncles, Kenneth

Cadenhead, has spent much of his life tracing our roots. His discoveries have given meaning beyond description to our name. Our family became intensely interested in our origin in Scotland. To our advantage, one of the benefits of such a strange name is that it makes tracing somewhat easier.

I mentioned earlier that some names were taken from the location of the family. That is exactly the case with our name. In the Borders area of Scotland, close to the village of Selkirk, there is a stream called Caddon Water. (Streams and rivers in Scotland are often called "Water.") Sometime around the fourteenth or fifteenth century, the families who lived around the head waters of Caddon Water became known as the clan of the Caddonheads. The result was that they eventually took that identity upon themselves as the name for their family.

The use of the locale as a way of creating a family name was not unique. Just as the families at the headwaters of Caddon Water claimed Caddonhead as their name, the people at the "foot" of the stream claimed Caddonfoot as their identity. In fact, today there is a village located where Caddon Water empties into the Tweed Water. The village is known as Caddonfoot.

A Dream Come True

All my life I have heard stories of how our family began long ago in Scotland, including this mysterious place at the head of Caddon Water. This past year while on sabbatical in Scotland, my wife and I had the opportunity to visit this area. We flew to the closest major airport, rented a car, and headed toward the southern part of Scotland, often referred to as the Borders Region.

Family members of my father's generation had made this journey previously, so I had the benefit of good directions and relatively recent maps. We drove on an old road that paralleled the Tweed Water and came to the village where Caddon Water emptied into the Tweed. It was the village of Caddonfoot. It had one small but modern, school, a church, and some homes. There was nothing surreal about it. But what made my visit to the village so powerful, even magical, was that here for the first time I saw Caddon Water. There was nothing normal about this first crossing of Caddon Water. Without knowing its history, it would have been no different than countless other streams flowing under bridges. It was just a small stream, not much to set it apart, except for one thing: It was the stream I had heard about all my life.

We followed a narrow road that wound its way alongside the stream, traveling against the flow of the stream. We followed Caddon Water as it slowly and gently made its way through several farms and down from an ever-increasing descent. As we traveled against the flow of the stream, we moved toward a high and mountainous area. The road passed through a gate, and there was the sign that I had waited to see for so many years. On the sign were the words "Caddonhead Farm." To this day, there is still a farm that surrounds the headwaters of the stream bearing the name of the family. A corporation now owns the farm, as is the case with many farms in Scotland. It is leased back to shepherds who use the hillsides to feed their sheep and cattle. The farm is a reminder of the people who, hundreds of years ago, took upon themselves the name of the stream that provided their water.

What might seem like trivia to anyone not named Cadenhead was for me an unbelievably powerful and sacred moment. To have the privilege and opportunity to stand where my family name originated six hundred years ago ranks among the high moments of my life. As I stood on that ground and drank from that stream, I thought of all the generations that preceded me. All of that history is a part of who I am.

No matter what I gain or lose in life, no matter how long or short my life may be, the name that identifies me is a gift. I did not simply appear at this moment by coincidence. I am a product of those who precede me, including families who once lived at the headwaters of this stream in a place far away from where I live now.

Our Name Is a Gift

Do we really appreciate the gift we have in our name? Granted, we had value in the plan of God and the bodily connection with our mother before we were given a name. We "were" before we had a name. But that does not take away the value and meaning of the name we were granted. In that name, we have a connection to the past that brought us into being.

Our name connects us to places, people, and the occupations of those preceding us. Even though it may have been given us after our creation, do not overlook how we are identified when our earthly life is over. We are remembered by our names. Names take on their own power. This identification is a special gift, and it is disassociated with anything we do. It is simply a part of who we are. Instead of appreciating it only as a way of separating your credit card from another, claim it as a gift, a part of your being.

Notes

[1] Kristine Elliott, "A Brief Introduction to the History of Names," http://www.sca.org/heraldry/laurel/names/namehist.html.

[2] Ibid.

[3] Ibid.

Chapter 10

Being:
Daily Checking
the Stock Report

"They do not labor or spin." —Matthew 6:28

As a minister and counselor, I am regularly approached by people with all kinds of problems. As with all ministers, the range of problems covers the spectrum. Many of the issues are predictable. Some of them, however, might surprise you. Nevertheless, one area of struggle that gets lots of "frequent flyer miles" relates to financial issues. Counselors often discover that financial stresses can indicate underlying issues, and the financial dimension is just one expression. Whether an isolated issue or the tip of an iceberg that lies deep within, those financial matters must be addressed. The issues range from young families who have trouble getting from month to month to owners of companies who are watching their businesses take frightening dives.

I am no financial expert, but I do work closely enough with people to know that the last ten years have been a financial rollercoaster for most investors. During the decade of the nineties, the economy was incredible, to the degree that it seemed difficult not to make money in the market. There was money to be made, and many investors realized enormous returns on their decisions. A lot of wise people got in and out at just the right time.

As money was being made, wide circles of people appeared to benefit, or so it seemed. Benevolent organizations used this period as an optimal time for gaining support. Not only did many benevolent agencies do well, but during this same decade there were significant increases in additional not-for-profit benevolent groups. The generosity of wise investors found its way into the needs of the community, including the church. I have no access to the numbers at this writing, but it would be interesting to get a picture of how many churches had major capital improvements during this period of time. Church after church added facilities, and many higher institutions of learning moved quickly during this time to garner support. There was an assumption within most benevolent groups and not-for-profits that it was a matter of making needs known so the money would appear. In many cases, it happened just that way.

More than a few of us bought cars we never thought we would own. Instead of lowering the cost of an automobile, manufacturers offered rebates on increasingly overpriced cars. Then, instead of continuing rebates, those same manufacturers offered zero-percent financing. You no longer had to go to the bank to borrow money.

Risky Business

One unseen and unappreciated outcome of the nineties was the way people took on their financial successes as the backbone of their personhood. The late, great coach Vince Lombardi once said, "Nothing breeds confidence like success." There comes a point when we cannot tell the difference between our sense of being and the wealth with which we have associated ourselves. Our wealth begins to define us and our ability to earn becomes the definition of who we are. There is little more dangerous about good times than the way we begin to take on our successes as an extension of our personality.

Not being a financial expert, I seldom offer solutions to complex financial problems. However, two signals indicated that we were navigating through strange financial waters. One was the zero financing of automobiles. I am not saying it was bad. It was simply a huge shift in the normal way of doing "auto business." It was a signal of new times. Suddenly the bank was not a factor in a common person's auto purchase. A simple thing, yes. But this trend had a flashing light on it that said a new day had arrived.

Toward the end of the nineties another issue signaled the imbalance of days to come. It was the recurring news of mill closings in communities around the country. These stories were not of places far away but close to home, in my case both logistically and figuratively. I live in Charlotte, North Carolina, and I recall in the late nineties several mill closings in areas around the edge of the metropolitan area. Whenever I raised concern, the response was almost always the same. Charlotte is a banking and financial center. Mill closings will be a blip on the screen at best, and Charlotte will never skip a beat.

I could not ignore these news stories for other reasons. One is that I am from a mill background, and I say that with a huge amount of pride. I grew up in a mill town and lived my life in a mill village. Huge numbers of people make their living in mill environments, and these normal, everyday people cannot just disappear when the mill closes. Another reason I was seriously bothered by the nonchalant attitude of closings is that hardworking, tax-paying, car-buying people live in mill areas. You can't shut mills down and not feel those vibrations in businesses far away. The average mill worker may not invest in large-scale property developments, and they may not be likely candidates for golf course communities, but they buy cars and milk and shoes and books. They borrow money to buy houses and send their children to college. I found it hard to believe that economic and community leaders could write off the passing of the textile industry as the price of progress.

I realize there are all kinds of reasons for the demise of longstanding ways of doing traditional business as we have known it. Some have said that NAFTA would have occurred even if the U.S. had not officially brought it into reality. Others claim that the immediate negatives of NAFTA will change into positive results over a long period. This remains to be seen. Yet, as a casual observer, one thing becomes clear. The post-modern era will be remembered for doing business in a new way. Old rules have given into a new set of rules that are currently written in pencil, not ink.

Financial and Emotional Confidence

As if that were not enough to change the mix of things, factor into the equation the widespread fraud and misrepresentation of reality. Think of how many times in the last few years the headlines have been filled with scandals in high places. The assumption is dangerously widespread in our society that top executives make numbers work to protect their position or inflate their personal worth, and the person who pays the price for those poor choices is the investor who trusted the company with savings over a lifetime. Without a doubt, integrity still characterizes many leading executives today, but a serious crisis of trust exists in our culture.

Then, as surely as the "hot doughnuts" sign had been on, it was switched off. A hot economy that had already begun to cool took on a new look as of September 11, 2001. So much changed after that day. If there was an age of innocence, it disappeared. I hear people debate about when the postmodern era actually came into being. Some lay it at the feet of the rather innocuous changing over to the new millennium. Others say it is the result of the World Wide Web. I do not deny the influence of many factors. Still, I think there will come a day when history will point with clarity to September 11, 2001, as the actual inauguration of the postmodern era.

A bubble burst that day, and it impacted the life of a country and world and emphatically influenced the lives of individuals in our country. Nothing was the same after that dreadful day. And it is an understatement to say that it dramatically influenced our checkbooks and mutual funds.

No Small Issue

The first thing I want to confess is that the way I offer limited advice to those under financial stress is different today than it was a few years ago. Not long ago, I would have resorted to clichés and poorly defined assumptions about working hard and trusting the system. Now, though, how do you tell someone to trust the system when the company that managed their retirement account betrayed them and their financial security no longer exists? Be careful about telling that person to trust the system.

The main reason I can no longer resort to clichés is that I know exactly how it feels to watch retirement funds diminish. Only a few years ago, it would not have been much of an issue. The reason is that I evidently did not have a lot of concern about retirement. If it had been an issue, I would have been preparing long before now. As with most people, age brings about changes in perspective that make one view life differently.

In retrospect, it seems like I awoke one morning around the age of fifty and realized I was terribly unprepared. Savings were minimal, and future retirement was not even on the radar screen. So I set out on a mission. We had previously used most of our funds for the education of our children, which was a privilege and pleasure. Now that education was a past need, I decided to address our future needs. I began at a late date to save all within my power.

My anxiety increased when colleagues shared how much they had already set aside for retirement needs. When I heard them speak of certain amounts of money already in the bank, I felt an indescribable anxiety over not having prepared. So we set out on a mission and begin setting aside as much as possible to make things happen. Well, timing is everything. Within the same period of time when I became serious about putting money into funds for retirement, the economy began signaling that a serious cooling down period was just ahead. I guess I should not have been surprised. As a matter of history, I have always bought high and sold low! The good news is that it has saved me much stress over what to do with the money I would have otherwise made.

Nevertheless, just about the time results began to show in my account, the stock market hooked up to the rollercoaster at Disneyland. I watched the numbers go up and down, mostly down. In terms of the bottom line, my numbers looked much like they did before I got serious. I don't fully understand the stock market. I can assume with some degree of certainty that money that was in my account is now in someone else's fund. I quickly developed an appreciation for something Will Rogers once said. He once commented that he was concerned about the return of his money. Not the return *on* his money, just the return *of* his money.

When your age and savings move in opposite directions, security is no longer an intellectual discussion. Security moves from your wallet to the heart, maybe the stomach. The flip side of this experience is that as a minister and counselor, I developed a deeper sympathy with people struggling to have an identity separate from their savings account. I still believe strongly that at some point, we still have to fall back on our faith in God's love and care. I still believe that if we are responsible with God's gifts to us and act as good stewards, somehow, someway, God will move in and do for us what we cannot do for ourselves. That is a journey from the head to the heart, a long distance to travel for full rest.

A Tough Question

The toughest challenge we face is how to claim a sense of being separate from what we earn and from what we have or do not have in savings. Do we have a sense of worth and value apart from the financial labels that define us? Too many of us equate our value with our latest mutual fund report. Defining ourselves in good times may not seem like a bad thing. Having resources at our disposal is a huge boost to our confidence. Yet, when those resources disappear, we may face an overwhelming identity crisis.

When I took on a serious attitude about my retirement account, I developed a bad habit of checking it almost every day. It takes only a few seconds to pull it up on the Internet. It was exciting at first. Then, as the economy began to cool, the bottom line began to drop. Even when I put money into the account every month, it seemed to drop more than it rose. Checking it became such a habit that my mood in the early part of the day depended on whether the numbers went up or down during the night.

A good friend of mine, who is well respected in the financial business, monitors my account. By now he must be sorry he offered to do that for me. After more than a few hand-wringing e mails to him with my questioning if we should make changes in the funds, he wrote me a message one morning that said, "Turn your computer off and quit checking your account every day." His advice was timely and wise. When we allow financial security to become a primary definition of who we are, the potential for obsession is likely.

Do not think I'm suggesting that we should not prepare. We are expected to be good stewards of our resources. In fact, the misuse of our resources often indicates other personal misapplications in our lives. However, when we act responsibly, follow good advice, and work hard, we have to let it go and trust the system and God's providential care.

Balancing responsible financial behavior on one hand and not being defined by it on the other hand requires careful attention. We have to be more than what our quarterly earnings statement reports about us. Larry Carroll is president of a financial firm in Charlotte and works with hundreds of people who are heavily invested. Larry offers this guidance about the way one balances responsibility without being obsessively defined by it:

> Fear and greed are not only the two emotions that motivate investors, they are the two powerful enemies of successful investing. When the market is going straight up, as in the late nineties, we extrapolate the values of our current assets into the future and conclude that not only will we be able to retire early, but that we can live lavishly in retirement.

My experience is that we also think we are taller, slimmer, a good singer, and that we can dance.

When the market crests the hill and goes down for a few years, as in 2000, 2001, and 2002, we immediately extrapolate our declining net worth to zero and conclude that we will never be able to retire and that our children will have to take care of us in our old age. Horrors! This manic depressive approach to investing not only leads us to bad investment decisions, but is reflected in our daily moods, how we interact with our family, and our sense of self-worth.

Markets have gone up and down since the beginning of time, and we continue to think, "This time is different." It is not different, and neither is the next time nor the time after that. The markets will go up and down every day, every month, and every year for the rest of your life. Learn to live with it. If you cannot separate your emotions from sound investing, you should hire a professional to handle the investments. That advisor should be able to bring reality to your retirement plan and then update that reality for the inevitable changes in the market.

More importantly, the retirement plan needs to be updated for the changes in your personal life that may have a bigger impact on your finances than the ups and downs of the markets. For example, the need to help your children get an education and get started in life. Recently a client called to tell me that his daughter was divorcing and that he was going to support her and her two children, his grandchildren, for the next year or so. This will dramatically change his retirement plans and impact his financial statement more than what the market does this year. But it needs to be done and is the right thing for him to do.

Things are never as good as they look at the top or as bad as they look at the bottom. The truth is in the middle. It is not important what the markets do over the next three months or the next three years. It is very important what they do over the next thirty years. Over the next thirty years they will go up and down. They always have and they always will. Put a plan in place that will let you stay focused on the thirty-year scenario, rather than what your latest 401(k) statement says.

Your core values do not change on a daily basis. Your self-worth does not fluctuate with the markets. Your relationship with your family should not change based what the Dow Jones Industrial average did today. Whether times are good or bad, you are not your financial statement. You and your mission are much more important than that! So get on with it! [shared by permission]

Another Perspective

While in a physician's waiting room recently, I read a magazine article by Suze Orman. She is a well-known author and conference leader who lectures about money matters. In this article, Orman mentioned two things that caught my attention. The first was in the byline of her article when she stated, "managing your finances is a spiritual challenge." I could not agree more. The way we manage our financial resources is symptomatic of other issues in our lives. Look at your checkbook and you will quickly see what is important to you.

Do you remember Jesus' encounter with the rich young ruler? What was really the issue here? The man's riches so defined him that he had no sense of being beyond them. His riches were not a means by which he could live out his sense of being. They *were* his being. They owned him. He could not separate himself from them.

The other thing that caught my attention was a story Orman shared about her father. She described her father's self-image as feeling like he was nothing without money. Her father owned a small business. One day it caught on fire. As he watched it burn, he ran into the flames and picked up his cash register. In it were only the receipts of one day. However, the hot metal left him with third-degree burns. Orman's summary statement says so much: "Thinking less of yourself because of finances will blind you to life's blessings."[1]

Enter this fact into your memory bank—we are more than what we read in our quarterly reports. We were people when we came into this world, and we had nothing. Checking the stock report every day may be okay as long as it is a business or even a game. But when it becomes the measure of our personhood, we tread on dangerous ground.

Note

[1] Suze Orman, "A Matter of Perspective," in *Guideposts*, ed. Edward Grinnan (New York), 15.

Chapter 11

Being: Fatigue, the Silent Opponent

He will not grow tired or weary. —Isaiah 40:28

The question was asked in an earlier chapter, "Who has time just to be?" We could raise another equally legitimate question: "Who has the energy just to be?" A clear awareness of being requires all our capacities, physically, mentally, and spiritually. It is difficult, if not impossible, to be fully engaged in a desire to be when we are preoccupied, even obsessed, with our physical condition. Often we are aware of our physical, emotional, and mental conditions, and then there are times when our physical condition overrides us without our awareness. It is difficult to be tuned into anything when we are tired.

The kind of fatigue that concerns me most today is not the acute state of weariness that comes from a single day or a short time of exertion. Instead, it is the chronic state of fatigue in which far too many people live these days. It is a state of exhaustion that places great limits on the human mind and spirit. Look around you and pay attention to the people you encounter each day. Look at their eyes. Pay attention to their expressions. Listen to what they are really saying beneath their words. Remember, God does not grow weary. Also remember that we are not God. We can become tired. If God had to rest, why do we think we should be able to ignore this common lot among so many of us?

Fatigue in a Leisure World

An intriguing contradiction is being played out before us in our culture. On one hand, we live in a society that claims to have bought into the leisure lifestyle. We go to great extremes in buying lifestyles that have leisure labels attached. Yet, being preoccupied with leisure and being rested are not the same. In fact, I know many people who stay exhausted trying to work out all their leisure requirements. At the least, leisure does not insure rest in our society. The bottom line is that too many people are walking the fine line of exhaustion, and often they are not even aware of it.

Personal Experience

I shared in chapter 3 my experience while on sabbatical in Scotland. I intentionally chose a place on a small island so that I could personally experience what it meant to be. I ached for a time of solitude, a time when I could be driven from within myself instead of by the normal demands of my external world. The island of Westray was about as close to the perfect setting as I could have desired. When I arrived, I felt like I had entered a monastery by the sea.

In solitude I awakened the first morning to the sound of silence. With the exception of the wind coming in from the water and an occasional car passing on the single-lane road between my room and the sea, the world was as silent as I could remember in a long time.

There were none of the usual sounds to which I would normally respond. There was no telephone close to my room. More than ever before, I experienced a sense of *being*. My host had prepared a comfortable room with only a bed and a table for writing. I had special books to read and a brand new laptop to use for the beginning of this manuscript. Finally, I would enter my laboratory of being. I anticipated my first day to be the most memorable and the most productive of all.

My First Day of Solitude

So, how did my first day of concentrated being go? I can best describe it with two words—frustration and struggle. My frustration came from the struggle just to stay awake. Without the normal demands that would otherwise command my attention, I could neither concentrate nor produce. I absolutely could not stay awake. The first lesson I would learn in my new laboratory was that I was far more fatigued than I realized.

My fatigue signaled more than the stress of a three-day trip. I realized that my deep weariness was the result of poor personal management over a much longer period of time. In my quiet room by the sea, I tried my best to be productive and focus on the mission that brought me there. I wanted to become engaged in meditative and reflective thought. Yet, time after time I simply shut down my laptop and lay in my comfortable single bed. There was no reflective thought, no quality prayer time, and no productive writing due to lack of focus, at least not on that first day. I had no idea just how tired I was. When the external stimuli that normally guided my day were taken away, I had little energy for anything within. Fatigue was an enemy I needed to recognize, identify, and commit to overcome. If silent fatigue was an enemy in my room by the sea, why should it be any different in less protected places? After a couple of days of resting, my ability to meditate and reflect slowly began to increase.

That experience was simple, but was there a larger lesson to be learned? If fatigue interfered with the level out of which I wanted to function in an isolated place, how does it work against reflective and meditative thought in the normal routine of living? I have no research to prove it, but my hunch is that most of us function regularly on the borderline of fatigue. We are pressed on every side. We seldom slow down; at least, we do not do so voluntarily. I believe fatigue is the enemy of developing an awareness of our sense of being. Who has time or energy to get beneath the obvious in our lives?

Obsessed with Speed

I am convinced that some of our fatigue is the result of a never-ending fast pace, a pace that is only getting faster. A few days ago I caught the end of a radio program on NPR. The speaker described himself as a speedoholic. I only caught the last few minutes and have no idea who the man was. But I was intrigued by his confession of being a speedoholic. Interesting name. In the part I heard, he described himself as being obsessed with getting things done in as short a time as possible. Life must move fast. If accomplishing a task is good, accomplishing it faster is better. Our culture is obsessed with speed, and I think that obsession will only increase. Our need to get life done in less time is already and will continue to extract a huge price. We are a culture of speedoholics.

Culture of Speedoholics

If a study were made of the "history of speed," I feel certain it would find its beginning with the industrial revolution. So much changed when products no longer had to be stamped, cut, and assembled by hand one at a time. Mass production became more than the label for industry. It became a way of life. Why take a week to build a carriage when you can build one in a day? Building two a day becomes the goal. Soon, the goal of speeding up production is discovered to be the way of wealth and prosperity. The seeds of speed may have been sown long before, but the industrial revolution fertilized the soil and brought it to life.

Fast forward to our time. Look at how the importance of speed has geometrically increased. Travel now allows one to eat breakfast and dinner on opposite sides of the ocean on the same day. Expressways moves us from point A to point B in a fraction of the time required a few decades ago. Our goal is to be mobile and get to our destination in as little time as possible. There is little emphasis on the journey. Just get us there!

More than in any other dimension of life, the information culture that surrounds us makes us think fast response and even faster retrieval of information are the marks of progress. We can go online and bid on an item sold in a foreign country. We can have it shipped overnight from nearly any place in the world. Distance means nothing because speed rules and moves everyone in the world closer.

We Want the World Brought to Us Now

Look at how we get our news. We watched the horrors of September 11th on television and saw them unfold at every nightmarish turn. The military actions that followed September 11th have been brought into our homes with unbelievable promptness, in many cases live scenes of the anguish of war. We do not have to wait to get the news. It is played out right in front of our eyes. We see it live. We want everything with an unforgiving expectation of speed.

We want our computers hooked to sources that send information back and forth immediately. "Dial up" will never again be fast enough. We want connections that make cables smoke. There is no way to know where the technical world will take us in terms of high-speed information. We have only touched the surface. If fast is good, faster is much better!

A High Price

My concern is that the high-speed pace of our lives and the high-speed expectation with which we approach life will have two diminishing effects upon us. First, some things cannot be subject to the expectation of speed. We cannot do the meditation and reflection our spirits crave in fractions of seconds. Contemplative life that is rushed with a time clock can never be more than symbolic.

The second diminishing effect is that living a life under the constant expectation of speed will eventually result in a deep and painful fatigue. The majority of the people I encounter today are suffering from weariness. And fatigue is the enemy of being! Encountering the mysterious presence of God will never happen when at the moment of sitting still, one falls asleep.

Our Lord called us to be faithful, and He called us to be disciples. He holds out the possibility for the abundant life. He did not call us to the mission of "burnout." If we know only the tight and rushed schedule of moving from club to shopping to soccer practice to dance lessons to PTA to board meetings to the golf course to the coffee shop, we will never have the energy to look within ourselves and get beyond the labels that define. Fatigue is an opponent of being.

Chapter 12

Being:
Facing the Giants

We seemed like grasshoppers in our own lives. —Numbers 13:33b

Push away all the forces that place their demands upon you. Separate yourself from all the noises that interrupt. Remove yourself from the barriers that normally provide cover. Relax and embrace solitude as a friend. Offer a centering prayer and think of what God must know about us, that part of us that we keep protected and carefully hidden away. We discover a vast, sometimes unfamiliar region, an inward land that we do not know well. As we sincerely respond to God's call to be, we might feel uncomfortably vulnerable. Without the normal things we depend on to define us, we may be looking at the future with different eyes. If you have been there, the future may look more than a little overwhelming. We may also discover that we are not alone, and not all the forces around us are pleasant and affirming.

If you have been there, you need no explanation. Maybe no one was aware of how you felt, but you knew you were in a different land. Not everyone moves into this land of solitude with ease. You may feel like you are one click short of red lining on the panic meter. It might be that you are there right now. Is there a word from the Bible that offers help in such a time? I want to answer that question by pointing you to two passages. One is from the book of Numbers and the other from Paul's letter to the church in Corinth.

The Land of Giants

Do you remember what happens in the familiar story found in Numbers 13? Moses sends spies into the land promised to the Israelites, but it is inhabited. A small thing called conquest stands between the children of Israel and settling in the home they are promised. The spies come back with differing perspectives. Only Joshua and Caleb see the opportunities. The others say, "We can't attack. They are stronger than we are." And the truth is that the enemies were sizable opponents. Keep in mind that this was not their imagination at work. More than likely, the people who held the land they were promised were frightening sights. "Why, we seemed like grasshoppers in our own eyes." But notice—"in our own eyes." It was a description of how they perceived themselves.

I find it interesting that they did not encounter giants until they got serious about what God had promised them. It seems to me that if it was what God had promised, they would not have to deal with giants. Just march in and say, "God sent us. So pack and get out." Obviously it does not work that way. They were doing what they should do, what God commanded them to do, and they encountered giants. It seems to me that if we do what is right, even what God commands, we ought not to have to deal with giants.

We could deal with a ton of theology at this point, but that is not where I want us to camp. I would like to let that exchange in Numbers 13 become a symbol of where many of us are today, the symbolism of feeling like grasshoppers in a land of giants. I ask again, "Is there anyone who can identify with that feeling?" Often as we approach solitude and silence, forces that seem enormous and intimidating confront us.

Giants Stalk Us

Giants represent great difficulties, and they stalk us everywhere. They are in our families, our churches, our social lives. They are real in our jobs. But most of all they exist in the quiet places of our hearts. Do you know what I mean when I refer to the hidden places of our hearts? Are there fears we never make public? Even the people who are supposedly closest to us don't know about them. We even try to hide some fears from God, which does not make sense. Yet, we try to do it nonetheless. When we pull away from the distractions and separate ourselves from the labels behind which we hide, these giants become clear to us. Then, more than ever, they begin to stalk us. We don't need anyone to tell us, but we know we must deal with these fears, these giants. We know we must overcome them or they will devour us. When we are haunted by the realities of life and even those within our own minds, how much better it would be if we could have the attitude of Joshua and Caleb. In effect, they told the others that they would be stronger by overcoming them. Don't you wish you could take that perspective, that you could become stronger by overcoming the giants that exist in your life?

A Faulty and Misleading Understanding

Many people believe the presence of God in a person's life and connecting with God in the most intimate way should keep them from all struggles and conflicts. I think a case could be made that being faithful to God and trying to do right often bring conflicts and struggles. I could not think of a better example than that demonstrated in the life of Paul. One might think that Paul, during his great missionary journey to Rome, would have been kept by God's sovereignty from the power of violent storms and the threats of his enemies. Yet the opposite was true. He endured one long, difficult struggle after another. He was tormented by certain groups of Jews, and faced fierce winds, poisonous snakes, and all kinds of hardships, enough to make most people back up and take another approach to life.

Even though he served a God of infinite power, he had to deal with these issues. He even narrowly escaped drowning by swimming to the shore at Malta. In fact, in retrospect, it appears that ever since he changed team jerseys on the Damascus Road, the conflicts in Paul's life never ended. The pressure on Paul was persistent, but from every conflict he always emerged victorious through the strength of Christ.

Paul's Way of Facing Giants

Paul offers no better description of how he approached life during those difficult times than the one in his letter to the church in Corinth. In his powerful, vivid language, he wrote, "We are hard pressed on every side, but not crushed; perplexed, but not in despair; persecuted but not abandoned; struck down, but not destroyed. We always carry around in our body the death of Jesus, so that the life of Jesus may also be revealed in our body." That is how he faced giants.

Paul's strenuous struggle was endless. It is almost impossible to translate into English the level of stress Paul felt in his effort to be obedient. Yet, in his letter to the church at Corinth, he gives five images that are helpful as we try to deal with the giants we meet every day. If only we could be familiar enough with these images to be able to pull them from our memory banks and keep them in front of us when we feel surrounded by giants. The value of these images is still as applicable today as when they were written.

(1) First, Paul gives a picture of his enemies completely surrounding him but not crushing him, pressed at every point but not hemmed in. There are all kinds of pressures on us, but we are never in so tight a corner that there is no way out. With Christ guiding our lives as we respond to God's call to be, there is always an escape route in the spaciousness of God. Can you sincerely believe that?

(2) The second image is that of being at our wit's end. The image Paul tries to build needs some explanation. Is there anyone who has not at

some point felt that they were out of options and did not know what to do? I love the language of that verse—"wits end but not hopes end." That statement is true because we are dependent upon One who has a perspective that we don't, who sees so much more than we do, who knows already how things are going to work out.

(3) The third image is that of being persecuted by humankind but never abandoned by God. The image is of the enemy in hot pursuit. Hard as it may be to understand, one of the most notable facts about the martyrs has always been that amid their toughest circumstances, they have had their most meaningful times with Christ. As you claim your call and right to be, can you believe that God will never abandon you when you face the giants?

(4) The fourth image is even more dramatic. For Paul, the enemy has overtaken him, struck him, and knocked him down. Yet, what he experiences is not the fatal blow. He is able to rise again. He has been struck down but not destroyed, or literally, overthrown but not overcome. The Christian is one who may lose a battle but knows the campaign is not lost. The supreme characteristic of Christians is not that they do not fall, but that every time they fall, they get up again.

(5) The fifth and final image is the one of our Lord Himself. His example offers the secret of His own life, and it is the honest and simple principle that life involves struggle, challenge, and even pain. One can argue all day whether it should be that way or not. The simple fact exists—life is simply that way. To respond to God's call to be will place us in a land of giants. Paul was well aware that the more a person tries to connect with Christ, the more one must share the risks of Christ.

A Fact Restated

Again, one might ask what this has to do with the reality of God's call to be. It has everything to do with that call. What is being, if not to separate ourselves from the labels that define us, the labels behind which we tend to hide? When we can no longer depend on these external labels, we become vulnerable to the fears we kept at great distance for so long. When we are open and when there is no wall behind which to hide, we may at first feel defenseless. The truth is that we are not left defenseless. To be is to find enormous comfort and security that comes from God. As always, being precedes doing.

When conflict comes and the battle takes place in our homeland, the potential is great to become discouraged, even to surrender. I have come to the conclusion that God has nothing worth having that is easily gained, for there are no cheap goods on the heavenly market. Difficult times and places are our schools of faith and character. I am convinced of a principle at this point. If we are to ever rise above mere human strength, it will more than likely be through the pains of struggle. That is not the bad news. In fact, it is the good news.

A Reminder

Claiming our sense of being and recognizing that being must precede doing does not mean our lives cease to go anywhere. That fact still remains that we are not incidental actors on a stage. We are all players in an important drama called life. Responding to God's call to be is claiming that fact. And one thing is for certain—a part of that drama is the presence of giants. God gives us grace and strength to be like Caleb and Joshua.

Being Is Claiming

Psalm 138 is attributed to David and describes his confidence that God will fulfill exactly what He planned for David's life. There is admirable, even desirable, strength of being in David. David has a profound sense of confidence that nothing will keep God from bringing about His divine intentions in David's life. As David describes his life, he knows that nothing will deter God. Even David's sorrow will not set aside God's plan. The anger David receives from others will not deter God. David has a sense of confidence that is not characteristic of most of us.

Part of God's "call to be" is a positive claiming of all the experiences that make up our lives, the good ones and the bad ones. It is not coincidental that many of those who reach the deepest sense of spirituality are those who have experienced great suffering. Often working against us is an idealistic notion that life is supposed to be free from suffering and trial. When we give up imagining castles in the sky, we can then recognize the inner presence of God and claim the strength, power, and confidence that result from the divine connection offered to us. We become less driven by the voices of others and more directed by the voice within us.

Francois Fenelon has written, "The heart that serves, and loves and clings, hears everywhere the rush of angel wings." Yet, just as we accept and claim the hard moments as a part of our call to be, we also must recognize the positive moments that make up our experience. Just as the difficult times shape us, so do the positive moments. They come as gifts and become part of our total experience. We should not forget them or feel guilty for experiencing them. If tough experiences give us courage and direction, good experiences give us energy and hope. Embrace all that you are. All these experiences come together to make you the truly unique creation God intends.

Chapter 13

Being: The Essence of What It Means to Be

"And unless you change and become like little children . . . ."
—Matthew 18:3

When I began writing this project nearly a year ago, I had lofty hopes of how it might conclude. In all honesty, I assumed that after wrestling with what it means to be and how God calls us to be, I would end with some type of theologically breathtaking discovery. My hope was that in coming to terms with God's call to be, I would discover an unknown region of the inner world and thus be the envy of theologians everywhere. Surely there must exist deep inside the soul a sense of being that cries out for discovery. Peeling away the layers would bring to light something that had never been exposed before.

Well, in retrospect, I was both wrong and right. I was wrong in that there was no highly sophisticated, inner reality within the soul, and I was also wrong on the point of this mystery being sophisticated and unknown. Yet, I was right in that there is something underneath the layers of profession, address, resources, and aging personal characteristics. It is not sophisticated or complicated. And, to be honest, it is not even unknown.

So, What Is It?

Peel away the normal layers of identity on which we depend to set us apart from everyone else. Is there something that is ours when we arrive in this world and that we never lose throughout our journey? The answer is yes, and it is so simple and obvious. Underneath it all is the reality of being a child of God. How could I have not seen it from the beginning? Are we not created with a spark of the divine in us? Do we not come from God just as we return to Him? Take away everything else we have, and this dimension of our existence does not change. Granted, we can elect not to recognize it and live accordingly. We can continue to live in such a way that all the other layers of identity completely cover it. Yet, this "childness" is the one dynamic of our being that does not change with the passing of years. We are no less God's children if we accumulate many years. We are no less God's children if we become totally incapacitated.

The loss of our jobs does not change it. Whether we have black ink or red ink in our bank accounts matters not at all. We derive our being from God. In Him we find our being. In Him we are most fulfilled and satisfied. It is because we are created for relationship with God and nothing else fulfills that childlike sense of identity.

Claiming Our Identity

There is but one solution to the sense of amnesia so characteristic of our culture today, even the culture of the religious faithful. It is to be found in stepping around what we seem to have forgotten somewhere along the way and relearning who we are. Quite some time ago, Dr. John Claypool began a sermon with a story symbolic of our dilemma.

At the end of World War I, the French Army found itself with in a difficult situation. Upwards of a hundred soldiers were suffering from amnesia because of shell shock and also due to a faulty record system. Not even the army knew the identity of these individuals. In every other way, they were healthy, and if they could only be returned to their families and their native surroundings, this in itself might quicken the return of their memories.

But how to discover their identities and get them back to their families? Someone came up with the idea of having an Identification Rally in Paris. It would be highly publicized throughout the country, and families with relatives missing in action would be encouraged to attend. The plan was adopted, and the moment finally arrived when thousands of people gathered in one of the great plazas of the city. A platform had been erected in the center where all could see, and one by one these men stepped up to a microphone and looked out anxiously over the crowd, saying, "Please, please, is there anyone here who can tell me who I am?" A reporter who covered the event said it contained as much high drama as the events of the war itself.[1]

The story and the scene are symbolic of our culture today. Is this not similar to what we have been doing from our first day, in fact, from the moment we emerged from our mother's womb? Are we not people in search of an identity? There is no question closer to the center of the human mystery than the question "Who am I?"

I must repeat some of what was said in chapter 2. There is no way to answer the question of identity without going back to the scene of human creation. In the Genesis account, there is the image of God forming humankind out of clay and breathing His own breath into this new creation. While we may have been formed from the earth, we have been given life by the breath of God. In this profound but simple scene, we have the answer to the question "Who am I?" We are connected to God by His own breath.

Ultimately Our Choice

We make the choice as to whether we claim that identity or not. We decide whether we affirm that relationship or not. We decide if we let habits and lifestyles interfere with that relationship and thus ignore or deny the one role that gives the only sense of being that outlives all temporary identities. Ultimately we make the choice of claiming who we are or denying the one quality that outlives everything about us. Yes, when you take away all the things we depend on for our identity, the only one that lasts is the reality of being God's child. That is exactly what it means *to be*. It means we wisely claim our identity as God's child. To what is God calling us? God is calling us *to be His child*. That call goes to everyone. Whether we claim it is up to us.

Jesus Has Been Pointing to It

How could we not see what Jesus was pointing to in the prayer we know so well, the Lord's Prayer? Too often we limit this model prayer to the proper ordering of our requests or the appropriate wording for our prayers. Yet, in what we refer to as the Lord's Prayer, Jesus has clearly taught us the basis of our being. He instructed us to pray "Abba Father." This is the language of a child to a parent. Even more specifically, it is the language of a small child. In placing that image before us, He was not attempting to insult us, only to show us how simple God's call is. It is as simple as a child lifting a voice to a loving parent. If we are to live out our call to be in the form of being God's child, nowhere is it more clearly described and confirmed than in the way our Lord taught us to pray.

Claiming this role should precede everything we do. It gives meaning to the most normal of activities and sustains us in the most difficult of tasks. This calling to be God's child is what we share in common. It is our link to one another. Otherwise, we are merely orphans sharing the same space with nothing that creates the basis for relationship.

Is that not what Jesus came to restore? He came to reopen the possibility for us to claim that role. Because of sin we found ourselves in a hopeless situation. There was deep within our souls a longing to be restored, but we could not get ourselves out of the mess we had gotten ourselves into. Don't ignore the fact that the people Jesus taught to pray this way had already demonstrated a desire for a relationship.

The One Dimension of Life

Claiming our call to be God's child is claiming a gift of grace. When we were born into this world, we did not choose our parents. We did not choose the time or the place. All the dimensions of our birth were gifts beyond our choosing. Of course, we may walk away from our heritage and deny our connections with family. Regardless, the first breath was a gift of grace. We did not order it or arrange it. So it is with our claiming God's call to be His child. It is a gift of grace. We have done nothing to earn it, and we lose it only by rejecting it.

Our "divine childness" precedes all other layers of identity that we add to our lives. No matter what happens to us in life, no matter what life takes from us, we cannot lose this identity that is underneath all the others. If the company pushes us out of our office, it does not change. If illness or age incapacitates us, it does not change. If everything around us goes through a transformation, this "divine childness" cannot be taken from us.

Of all the good things that may come our way, nothing gives meaning to life to the degree that being God's child offers us. To be that child gives significance to our "doing." For that reason, "being" precedes "doing." It is simple and easy. Nothing else matters as much. And it is placed right in front of us when Jesus tells us to pray by opening our prayer with "Dear Father"—more specifically, "Dear Daddy."

Note

[1] John Claypool, *Who Am I?*, sermon preached at Northminster Baptist Church, Jackson MS, 9 September 1979. Used by permission.

Chapter 14

Being: What We Need Most

"I will not let you go until you bless me." —Genesis 32:26

In the previous pages I have tried to articulate some of my own struggle to be and where that journey has taken me. I have operated on the assumption that I am not alone and that others believe our existence is more than just the superficial things that characterize us. One of my concerns is that some may perceive our responding to God's call to be as a passive experience, something we just sit and wait for until it takes place in our lives.

After all, have we not already concluded that the essence of being is claiming our place as God's child? Are we not born with that status, needing only to claim it? In describing the dynamics of this struggle of the soul, I may have underemphasized how much of a struggle it can be. For some people, the joy that comes from claiming one's sense of being may be in direct proportion to the degree of struggle involved.

Even though it comes as a gift, it must be something we are determined to claim. If you know personally this struggle of the soul, my best advice is to do more than just claim it. Instead, be determined to hold on to it.

When I think of the level of determination needed to claim that sense of being, one story continually comes to mind. It is the story of Jacob and his wrestling match at Jabbok. The story is found in the thirty-second chapter of Genesis. The account is filled with numerous images, but one image emerges as dominant. It is the image of a man who in spite of his many faults had an indomitable desire to have his life blessed by God. Is that not what so much of our struggle to be is about—a genuine desire to feel that we have God's blessing? If we peel away the identifying labels and accept the fact that underneath them we are simply God's children, is that not what any child wants, to be blessed by one's parent, especially one's Divine Parent?

A Story of Determination

I hope you are asking how this story could possibly relate to our desire to be. Put together a list of Scripture passages that qualify as head-scratchers, and this passage would be right on top. The story is about Jacob, and what we tend to remember most is Jacob's mysterious struggle with God. When I read of Jacob and this strange wrestling match, I find myself being terribly familiar with this unusual experience. As we conclude this journey together, Jacob's experience can become instructive for us.

Jacob's entire life was characterized by trying to make things work to his advantage. From the time he came from his mother's womb, he struggled for something that would fill the empty places of his soul. He connived his way into his brother's birthright, which in that day was no small piece of theft. He moved on to encounter Laban and would almost meet his match, although eventually getting what he wanted. Jacob was a doer. He fits the profile for one who evidently defined himself by possessions, power, and prestige. For Jacob, whose name means the supplanter, nothing stood in the way of his getting what he needed. He became an image of ambitious success. Yet, clearly, an image is created of a self-initiating, type A individual that no amount of human maneuvering would satisfy the longings of his soul. What he needed most could not be confined to the typical definitions of his day.

Even though we remember this story most because of Jacob's struggle with God, a number of struggles are part of the landscape of Jacob. There are leftover issues from beating his brother out of his birthright. He then went to the far country and had a struggle with Laban in a deal that ended up with marriage to the wrong woman. Finally he got his wish, the wife he desired. He made his fortune and was on his way back to his brother's land to bring an end to the dispute. The end might even require Jacob's life.

Still Something Missing

In spite of this ambitious and successful man's accomplishments, there was another internal struggle, something all of his doing could not satisfy. Jacob longed for something deeper in life, an obvious desire that needed to be addressed. This man was wrestling with himself long before we read of his struggle with the stranger who, by the way, turned out to be God.

The famous wrestling match is described in half a verse—not a lot of space for something so well known. Some scholars have considered the possibility that a piece of the early manuscript somewhere along the line omitted several verses. The story may have been shortened a bit and included only what we now have, the details we need to know.

What we do know is that there is a seemingly complicated man named Jacob who encounters a mysterious stranger. The stranger somehow, someway became symbolic of what Jacob needed most. Who was the antagonist who came out of the dark? The stranger was not Esau, Jacob's imagined opponent. His antagonist was not human. Instead, this one who appeared was the Almighty God who would force Jacob into a moment of reckoning. We have a simple description of a man who wrestled, could not prevail, touched Jacob's hip, and permanently knocked it out of joint. This stranger eventually blessed

Jacob, which is exactly what Jacob needed most. In fact, he had been needing it and searching for it all his life.

The Labels of the Past No Longer Satisfied

Here is Jacob, one who had always evaded the truth about himself, leaning on labels that are as familiar to us today as they were to him long ago. By way of one strategy or another, Jacob had outwitted almost everyone—his brother, his father, his uncle. That is the way *doers* work. He had maneuvered and manipulated his way to the goal of having life exactly as he desired. And what had it brought him? No peace, no contentment. I have to believe that Jacob also understood life as overshadowed by guilt. And here he is, encountering the one person in life that is the opponent in so many of our struggles and wrestling matches—God! He would now experience firsthand a reckoning with God. When the mysterious antagonist touched Jacob's thigh and would not let him go, it was a symbol of the fact that Jacob was in the grip of a power far beyond himself. The story describes Jacob as not letting the stranger go. They wrestled all night and just as the stranger sought to leave, Jacob held on and would not let go without his blessing. Even if Jacob was not aware of what he needed most, something within him took over and refused to give up.

I wonder if we all have not been there, knowing we need something more than what we are getting from all the struggles that fill our days and nights. Stripped of former labels, Jacob could not rely on previous ways of defining himself. It is clear that for all outward definitions, he had done well since his departure from the family place. The image portrayed of Jacob is that of a successful man. He had two wives, two women servants, and eleven sons. We have no account of his daughters, but surely there were some. None of this provided the ultimate value he desired. His possessions could not satisfy his needs.

No wealth, no possessions, no props of former confidence could sustain him in these moments. It was a time when he could only be defined by that which was deep in his soul. As we all eventually discover, there are times in our lives when all we have accumulated cannot help us. Our "things" can only help us so far. Who are we underneath all these labels? Recognizing and claiming that basic element of our individual lives is often discovered only after the struggle of the soul.

Defined by the Past

Haunted by his history, Jacob had a past that sought to define him. His path had not always been one of integrity. Jacob had a way of getting what he wanted, whether it fell within his moral rights or not. On this night of Jacob's struggle, he knew all too well the sin that separated him from his brother Esau. As much as he might try to forget all he had done in past years, his past continued to define him.

There were old memories and old fears. He had to submit to that which he could not change. No amount of craftiness or creativity could change reality. Regardless of how successful he might appear, Jacob knew these labels were worthless in his struggle of the soul. His world was shadowed by guilt and colored by the past. Surely there was more to his life than all the memories he dragged with him to the ford of Jabbok. Would there ever be peace in the deep places of his soul? He longed to be blessed, and he won the blessing not by being passive but by clinging. Do you see the powerful picture in this story? Jacob locks his arms around the neck of his mysterious opponent and holds on until he receives what he needs.

Are We Willing?

Are we willing to move beyond being passive about our call to be? The blessing we long for will not come by adding layers of labels to our lives. What we need most from God is simple. We need His blessing. Maybe we can learn from Jacob when he says to this mysterious stranger, "I will not let you go unless you bless me" (Gen 32:26). If we are called to be God's child, what can be more important than being blessed by this same Mysterious One?

Two important factors were to Jacob's credit. The *Interpreter's Bible* describes them this way: "The first was his awareness that life has a divine meaning above its material fact—the awareness that made him seek the birthright and made possible his vision at Bethel. The second quality, revealed here in his wrestling, was his determination."[1] He had struggled all night until he was hurt and in agony, but Jacob held on. Caught in the grip of life, his prevailing desire was not for escape. He still believed that what he needed was within reach.

A particular piece of this story has always been especially intriguing to me. There must be a lesson in the fact that the one with whom Jacob wrestled never overcame him, never prevailed over him. Jacob was like a grand stallion. Seemingly, it was not God's desire that Jacob roll at His feet. Jacob was no better off if he arrived at the end of this experience as only a groveling man with a hip out of joint. The picture we are given of Jacob as he finally meets his brother Esau is a man who, though walking with a limp, is at peace with himself. He seems to have been cut loose from his manipulating past and no longer afraid of a future that has images of a betrayed brother looming on the horizon.

We know Jacob's life changed after this experience. The man who had been known for his struggling, conniving approach to life became a classic example of a life of faith. There must be something to this blessing, something that changes life for the one receiving the blessing. If you follow Jacob from this moment on, his life is entirely different.

A Moment of Honesty

How many of us have been at Peniel, the place of wrestling matches? In what ways are you wrestling with God right now? The chances are good that, like Jacob, we may be wrestling with the regrets of our lives, our fear of the future, or the ten thousand "what ifs" that cloud the horizon. We are struggling with ourselves and we are struggling with God.

The answer to so many of our struggles is to claim who we were meant to be, God's child. In reality, it is a matter of letting God be God and allowing ourselves to be His child. Underneath all the labels on which we depend for our identity, we are simply children. Peel back the layers we use to define ourselves, and what we discover is not complicated. We need and want most to be blessed as a child of God.

When we experience that blessing, lots of things that previously concerned us do not seem so important.

Losing Is Winning

During my seminary days I was fortunate to have Dr. John Claypool as my pastor. I remember a sermon he preached on Jacob's struggle, and he concluded with a story that has stuck in memory for more than three decades. It was a story out of Nikos Kansautzakis's book *Report to Greco.* It seems that a young religious seeker made his way to the strip of land on the coast of Greece known as Mount Ethos, where for more than a thousand years holy men and hermits had lived in isolation seeking to know the deepest truths of God. This young man stopped one day and asked a hermit, "Say, old man. Do you still wrestle with the devil?" "Oh no," replied the old holy man, "I am too old for that. I now wrestle with God." The young man's eyes widened with wonder, and he exclaimed, "With God! Do you hope to win?" The old hermit said, "Oh no, my son. In this wrestling match I am hoping to lose."

Life can become so complicated, or so it seems. Yet what we need most is simple, and it is at the base of much of our struggle. The answer to our deepest longing is not more of the labels we use to define ourselves. What we need is to hold on to God until He blesses us as His child. Underneath it all, that is who we are. That is what we need most. We are born into this world as God's children. This is all we have when we appear. It is all we take with us when we go. Our peace and meaning is found in making our claim as child, and it is an identity no one can take from us. We must refuse to give up until we are identified as God's child.

As the young man said to the old holy man, "You are wrestling with God? Do you really hope to win?" And the old man said, "Oh no, this wrestling match I am hoping to lose." May it be so with each of us.

Note
[1] Cuthbert Simpson, *Genesis,* The Interpreter's Bible (Nashville: Abingdon Press, 1952), 724.

Epilogue

by Leighton Ford

Short Flights and Quick Returns

I am sitting on a bench at Lost Lagoon, on the edge of the hundreds and hundreds of acres of trees and trails that make up the vast Stanley Park in Vancouver, Canada. Behind me are the tall buildings of the city. Surrounding the park on three sides are the waters of English Bay and Burrard Inlet. In the background hover clouds over the mountains that frame Vancouver—my favorite city in the world.

At least it is my favorite city to visit. It is a lazy mid-summer afternoon, and I am here for an annual retreat, alone on my spectator's perch except for a few ducks in the grass by the water's edge, several bicycle riders on the path behind me, and several couples walking hand in hand around the lagoon.

My eye is drawn to the fountain spouting up in the center of the lagoon; from there I see a flight of birds take off in a perfect V-formation. They disappear, then in a few minutes come circling back, and still in formation splash down, their legs extended like the landing gears of the seaplanes at Coal Harbor nearby

"Hmm," I think, "short flights and quick returns."

As I watch their flight and muse on its symbolism, a seagull comes and sits just by my foot for a minute or two as if to say, "Pay attention now. This show is for you to notice."

It is a message from the birds! My thoughts go back to the time when I began a new ministry of spiritual mentoring for young leaders. At our very first board meeting the chairman asked me two penetrating questions: the first, what can *you* do that is unique? My answer was to springboard young leaders into their calling, with a gospel that is full and whole.

His second question was even more pointed: do you think you are doing something significant *only* when . . . or *mostly* when . . . you are traveling, going someplace?

That question went straight to my heart. So much of my life has been spent in going—to more than forty countries in my evangelism work. Now that needs to change.

My mission statement these days is to be an "artist of the soul and a friend on the journey." That will happen only as I learn both to be still and to go (or grow) deeper. In the words of T. S. Eliot about "old men," I need "to be still and still moving." Although I do not feel old at all, I realize mission for me will mean not always being on the go. There will be—like the flight of the birds—short flights and quick returns.

For many years my life was made up of catching flights to different places, eager to go, always even more eager to return home. Now I realize not only were these two ways I spent my time, but they are a response to two notes in my own song: the lure of the road and the call to home.

Across time these two longings were reflected in two phases of my career. For thirty plus years, my life was that of an active evangelist and leader. Now my calling focuses on being a spiritual director, or mentor. That first phase I suppose was very much a time of "doing for God." This second phase is much more that of "paying attention to what God is doing" in my own life and in the young leaders with whom I have the privilege of being a spiritual friend.

The heart of my time with these younger men and women is to listen together to God—to pay attention to what God is doing in their lives and mine. We seek together for what Al Cadenhead so well describes in this book, taking time to wait and to discover the "essence of being"—what is so often underneath our public lives.

I have noticed in my own life how my ministry journey and my personal journey intertwine. What God is doing in both is similar, very much like the interweaving of the intricate strands that are woven into a Celtic cord, a work of art designed to show how God is at work weaving the inner and outer parts of our lives into a whole pattern.

I want these younger men and women to pay careful attention to where their inner and outer selves disconnect, and where they need to come together in a beautiful pattern that reflects Jesus—the one whose inner life with his Father and whose outer life ministering to the crowds was very much one.

There is so much in our world that calls all of us to be busy, doing, active, never stopping to be still and listen to the inner voice of our calling. We live distracted lives in a distracting world. There is a huge need for us to heed the clear, calm voice of Jesus that says to us, as he said to his friend Martha who was busy fixing the meal when he came to visit, "Martha, Martha, you are anxious about many things. One thing is needful." And that one thing was to stop bustling and to sit and listen to him as her sister Mary was doing.

At the top of best-seller lists has been the popular book *The Purpose-Driven Life*. It is a good book that has helped many. And God knows I have no quarrel with having purpose! Being "purpose-driven" is a whole lot better than being "purposeless." But what I want for myself and others is a *purpose-drawn life*—one not driven by inner compulsions or captive to outer expectations, but drawn by God's own voice of love and wisdom.

A friend who is involved in raising funds for cancer research told me that she had never felt more "driven" in her life. (She knows she can be very compulsive at times.) But as I listened to her I sensed a different note. "I don't think you are driven in this cause," I said. "I think you are being drawn. You are listening to your own inner sense and using your gifts for a great need, and you are finding joy in doing so. I think you are being drawn by God's calling!"

There are seasons of our lives—there have been of mine—in which we are more active, more outwardly focused, more driven if you will. And hopefully as we become older there are seasons in which we become more reflective, when we move more from the "action" mode to a "wisdom" mode, assuming we have learned some wisdom from our actions, both good and bad!

This shift is normal in the pattern of our aging and maturing. Yet there are also critical moments at various stages on our journeys, times of earthquake and upheaval, in which we become more attuned to the "still, small voice" of God and of our own souls. Most of us need some kind of spiritual "jolt" to make us stop and listen long enough to pay attention to what God is saying to us.

For our daughter Debbie, it was a return bout with breast cancer that provided the jolt. Shortly after she learned that she had to face five months of aggressive chemo and radiation, she was out on her regular exercise run, dealing with the turmoil and fears in her spirit. She told me that on her run she had seen a "burning bush" plant in bloom by the roadside, and her mind had gone to Moses' burning bush experience when God called him.

"Do you think God has a special call for me?" she asked. "I have been searching for years as to what God has in mind for me. I don't want it to be on committees anymore!" The treatments are ended. The cancer seems to be gone. Deb is feeling and looking well and lovely. But most importantly, I believe she has also found her calling. For years she has loved putting together beautiful designs and colors for interior design. Now she has set up her own small business, has her license, and is helping her first client.

I told her recently, "Deb, this is what you have been made to do. I really believe this is God's calling for you. Your love of beauty, your eye for color, your creative instincts—all are being used. This is your vocation. You are 'letting God's glory through' as the poet Hopkins said we all are called to do!"

The writer Parker Palmer has described a time of depression that for him became a breakthrough. He points out that the word "depress" means to push down, and he pictures his depression as a figure following him for years, trying to get his attention. The figure finally had put a hand on him, "depressed" him, not as a punishment, but a call to discover the deepest meaning of his own life.

I think the poet Rilke must have had these dark times in mind when he wrote, "I love the dark hours of my being. My mind deepens into them."

To say I love the dark hours is too much. But I do know that for me the painful gift of grace has come during the dark days. There was an unexpected depression some years ago that came just after I had completed major leadership projects. Without warning, I was overcome with a sense of terrible inadequacy. During a series of meetings in Tulsa, Oklahoma, I was afflicted with a dark sense, a fear that nothing I had to say would matter to anyone. Even though I knew the gospel I presented was true, I had to force myself to carry out my assignments, and inwardly I was struggling.

One morning when I was scheduled to speak at a local university, I got on my knees and told God I could not go. "I am afraid of what they will say, or how they will receive what I say. I don't think I have anything to say that will make reach them." In that moment words of the Bible came to my mind—God's promise to Abraham, when the Lord asked him to leave his home and go into an unknown land. Abraham was frightened at the prospect, and the voice of God came to him: "I am your shield, and your exceeding great reward."

I do not know how those words came into my mind right then. I had not read them in a long time. But I realized they were also God's word to me. "Go out there, Leighton," he was saying. "I will protect you. And however people may react, your reward will be in knowing that you are mine!" I did go. I did speak, though I do not remember much of what I said. People may have been helped. But the one who was helped most was me!

I realized that my emotional paralysis had come in part at least because I was afraid of losing my identity. From the time I was sixteen, I had done a lot of public speaking. I was known as a communicator, an "evangelist." If that was taken away, who was I? In my heart I sensed God saying, "Leighton, you matter to me not because you are a good speaker or evangelist. I made you. I love you. I value you—not for your communication skills but because you are my son!"

Several months passed before that depression was gone. But those words stayed with me. And it seemed as if the very hand of God—that unseen hand that as Palmer says may press us down to get our attention—had also lifted me up with a new sense of what it meant to be stripped down and opened up before the face of God, and to know myself as loved by God more deeply than ever before.

What I want most now is to "still and quiet my soul, as a weaned child with its mother" so that my spirit is as "a weaned child within me" (Psalm 133), to be just Leighton, a loved son, father, husband, grandfather, friend, and above all friend of God.

Postscript.

After I finished the above, I realized that something else needed to be added. I went straight from writing to a luncheon concerning reconciliation, an area of ministry to which I am very committed. As I listened to friends sharing their vision, I was moved. I want to be involved! And I will be. As long as I live, I want to find mountains to climb for God!

So I remind myself that "doing" is still important. Action and reflection are not enemies, but friends! True doing is always rooted in a right "being" with God. As Robert has put it, "Much of our doing does not spring from our being. Instead of expressing our being our doing often disguises it. When our being is firmly rooted in Christ, our doing will no longer mask our being. It will be as good fruit springing from a good tree rooted in soil which is good."

I like that! And it leads me to pray, "Dear God, You have called me both to be and to do. May my very being always be rooted in Your love. And may my doing always express Your deep love. And may both my being and my doing let all your glory through! Through Jesus Christ my Lord, whose being and doing always reflected your glory. Amen."

Leighton Ford
President
Leighton Ford Ministries